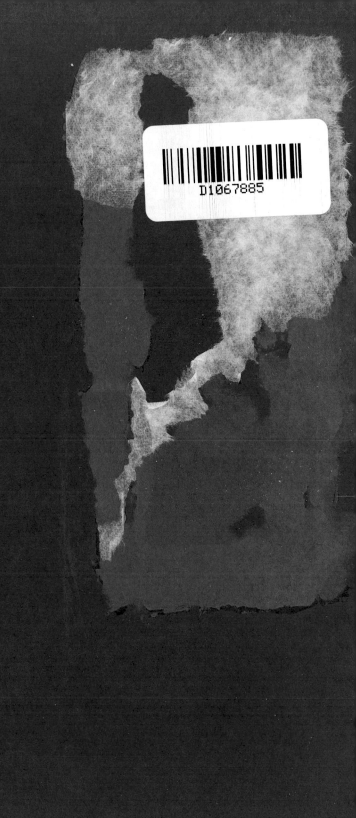

THE CABINET

STATE · TREASURY · DEFENSE · POST OFFICE · JUSTICE

INTERIOR · AGRICULTURE · COMMERCE · LABOR · HEALTH, EDUCATION AND WELFARE

SEAL
NOT YET
ADOPTED

HOUSING AND URBAN
DEVELOPMENT

THE CABINET

GERALD W. JOHNSON

illustrated by
LEONARD EVERETT FISHER

WILLIAM MORROW AND COMPANY

New York 1966

CONTENTS

ILLUSTRATIONS

THE CABINET TODAY

There is not one word about the President's Cabinet in the Constitution of the United States. Nevertheless, the President does most of his work through assistants, and people call ten of the most important assistants the Cabinet. That is all. There is no law about it; it is merely a custom.

Before the Constitution was written, when Congress was the whole government, the work had to be divided among several departments. So the makers of the Constitution took that system for granted. They simply said that the chief officer of each department should be appointed by the President and should give a written report to the President whenever it should be required; except that the officer who handled the government's money must also give a report to Congress whenever Congress should ask for one.

Other countries, especially Great Britain, France, and Germany have Cabinets, too. But, except for the name, they are hardly at all like ours.

The difference is shown by a story that is told of the great President Lincoln. It is said that after a certain question had been talked over, it was put to a vote. Every member of the Cabinet voted no. Then the President said, "You have all voted no but I vote aye, so the ayes have it." Under our system Cabinet officers may give their opinions— indeed, the law says that they must give their opinions when the President asks for them—but the final decision is made by the President alone.

If the President decides everything, we may wonder why he has a Cabinet. The answer to that is that the President doesn't decide everything, only very important things. There are thousands of small matters that must be looked after every day, but there is no need to bother the President with them. In most cases the law is so plain that a minor official can say, "This is what must be done," and that ends it. It is only when nobody knows what is best that the President must decide.

It is not so in England. When a very important matter comes up in England, the Cabinet sits as a committee to decide it. The prime minister is chairman of the committee, but he cannot overrule the votes of the other members; if he tried it, they would resign and the prime minister would have to form another committee. If he couldn't, he would have to resign himself. As the English say, "the government would fall."

Today there are eleven regular departments in the Cabinet, as well as many independent agencies not included in any department and reporting to the President directly, not through a secretary. As this book was written the eleven departments were as follows.

State, whose secretary is regarded as the first officer of the Cabinet. In many other countries this officer is called the foreign minister, because his work is to deal with foreign relations. For that, he has authority over all American ambassadors and ministers in foreign capitals. In Washington he deals with the ambassadors of other countries.

If one of them has something important to tell the President, he first calls on the Secretary of State, who then arranges for the ambassador to see the President. The secretary himself handles all ordinary business.

 Treasury, whose secretary ranks next after the Secretary of State. The Secretary of the Treasury handles all matters that have to do with money, which means that he has a wide variety of duties. He collects the taxes, of course, and pays the government's bills. He works on problems of exchange, debts, and payments and balances with foreign nations. The greater part of his business is done with banks and other institutions that handle large sums of money, such as insurance companies and brokers. He also has a small army of detectives in plain clothes, called the Secret Service, whose main duty is to run down counterfeiters, makers of false money. He has a small navy, called the Coast Guard, that gives help to ships in trouble at sea, but whose first job is to prevent smuggling, that is, bringing in foreign goods without paying the duty that the Treasury Department collects.

Defense, whose secretary, under the President, commands the Army, the Navy, and the Air Force. This department was called the War Department in Washington's day. Later it was split into War and Navy, with a secretary each. But after the Air Force was separated from the Army and Navy it was combined again into the Department of Defense. It is peculiar in that it has a secretary in the Cabinet and three other secretaries—of the Army, of the Navy, and of the Air Force—who are of high rank, but not in the Cabinet. Today the Secretary of Defense is no longer either a soldier or a politician. He is first of all the biggest business-man in the world. He has more than three million people on his payroll, a million not in uniform, and he does a business of about fifty billions a year.

Justice, whose head is the Attorney General, a member of the Cabinet, but not called a secretary. In the beginning he was merely the President's lawyer, but the President today has his special counsel, and the Attorney General's job is to enforce all Federal laws except martial law, which belongs to Defense, and the monetary laws, which are enforced by Treasury.

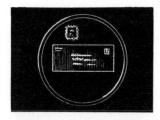

Post Office, not made a separate executive department until 1872. Its head is a Cabinet member, and is called the Postmaster General.

Interior, actually older as a department than the Post Office. The job of the Secretary of the Interior is to look after all government property not on foreign soil and not in charge of some other department. The government has so much property, of so many kinds, in so many places that a list of everything that the Department of the Interior looks after would make a whole book. Usually we forget the other things and think of the Secretary of the Interior as the man who takes care of the public lands, such as the great national parks and forests, the Indian reservations, and places where famous events have occurred. Three spots in his charge have been seen by millions of Americans;

they are the Washington Monument and the Lincoln and Jefferson Memorials.

Agriculture, the oldest, except the Post Office, of the government's public services. It was not a separate department until 1882, however, and its secretary not a member of the Cabinet until 1889. The work of the Secretary of Agriculture is to make sure that Americans are adequately fed and clothed. To do this work he employs more people and spends more money than any other department except Defense.

Commerce and Labor were one department from 1903 to 1913, but then they were separated and the secretary of each became a member of the Cabinet. Commerce is interested in business, which means that it has to do mainly with employers. Labor looks after all workers except farmers.

Health, Education, and Welfare was set up in 1953. Its name explains what the secretary does. Today there is a strong demand for a Department of Education, separated from Health and Welfare.

Housing and Urban Development, which was created in 1965. It deals with the special problems of cities, as most Americans now live in cities.

President Washington seems to have regarded the Vice-President as a member of the Cabinet, but that idea was dropped until President Eisenhower revived it, and Presidents Kennedy and Johnson followed. Still, the Vice-President is elected by the people, while the secretaries are chosen by the President, which makes a difference. If the President dosn't like what a secretary is doing, he can fire him, but he can't fire the Vice-President.

These officers are the ones that make up the Cabinet. Each member is supposed to look after a certain part of the government's work, but no member runs his department just as he pleases. He is an agent of the President. If he is an able man—and all Presidents try to get able men—he will be let alone most of the time. But if anything of great importance comes up, the President, not the secretary, decides what shall be done.

Yet they are great officers of state, and the law provides that if anything should happen to the President and the Vice-President, the Secretary of State shall become President. If he dies or resigns, the other department heads assume the Presidency in the order in which they are named in this book. However, that eventuality has never arisen.

The Cabinet has not always been organized this way. How it began and what part it has played in the history of the country make a confusing but fascinating story.

WASHINGTON'S CABINET

When Congress started to arrange for the President to exercise the executive power, nobody could be certain how the arrangements would work out because they had never been tried before. Separation of powers among the legislative (power to make laws), the judicial (power to decide what the law means), and the executive (power to make people obey the laws) was something new in the history of nations. The wisest men in Congress could only guess what would happen. Naturally there were widely different guesses, but on one point almost all were agreed.

This agreement was that the President must not have a Cabinet.

That sounds funny a hundred and seventy-five

years later, but in 1789 the men in Congress were perfectly serious about it, and with what seemed to them a good reason. The reason was that the word *cabinet* meant to them something that they disliked and that they were determined not to have. It meant, or at least it suggested, government by favorites.

For the legislative branch there was a sort of model in Parliament, and for the judiciary there was another in the king's courts of law. But for the executive the only model was the king, and that was precisely what the men of 1789 did not want. At the time the Cabinet seemed to Americans one of the worst parts of kingly rule.

Today the British Cabinet is the government, and rule by the Cabinet is regarded as the opposite of rule by the king. But it wasn't so in 1789. Parliament had not yet secured control of the government, and the House of Commons had not secured control of Parliament. The king was still clinging stubbornly to his divine right, and he still dared to choose his ministers, or some of them, regardless of what Parliament might think of them.

One of the original meanings of *cabinet* is a small room. In the old days a king's palace had a small room kept as a study, where the king could

read and write without interruption. It was called his cabinet, and a servant brought to that room anyone to whom the king wished to speak privately. A few of the king's advisers were called into that small room much more frequently than the others. In the course of time everyone talked of the Cabinet Council, and its members became more and more powerful.

If the king was wise, he put wise men in the Cabinet Council, and the kingdom was well ruled. But a foolish king was likely to prefer smooth flatterers, who often managed public business stupidly and dishonestly. Since really wise men were no more common among kings than among other people, it often happened that the Cabinet Council included men who were not honestly serving the king or the country, but getting whatever they could for themselves. So as the years passed the word *cabinet* came to mean, in many people's minds, a set of grafters and thieves who misruled and robbed the country.

Still, Americans recognized when they set up their government that the President had to have helpers and advisers. As he was to get the credit or the blame for what they did, it was only fair to let him select them. However, there was one check

on this power. If he chose a man notoriously unfit
for the job, the Senate could refuse to confirm him,
and the President would have to name another.

When Washington took the oath as the first
President of the United States in 1789, Congress
gave him only three departments—one to deal with
other nations, called the State Department; one
to handle the government's money, called the
Treasury Department; and one to look after the
defense of the nation, called the War Department.
Congress also allowed the President to hire a
lawyer to advise him as to what the law said about
particular cases. This lawyer was called the Attorney General, but he was not the head of a department. However, Washington was a careful
man. Whenever he called the department heads
together to discuss a problem, he had the Attorney
General sit with them to make sure that the solution they worked out was according to the law.
So it is usually said that the first Cabinet consisted
of four members.

To the State Department Washington appointed
Thomas Jefferson, who had been minister to
France and knew a great deal about foreign affairs.
To the Treasury Department he appointed Alex-
ander Hamilton, who had been one of his aides

during the war and who had written the greater part of *The Federalist*. To the War Department he appointed Henry Knox, who had been one of his generals during the war and had since managed military affairs under the Articles of Confederation. As Attorney General he named Edmund Randolph, a lawyer who had been governor of Virginia.

Each of these men had been known to Washington for years and he respected their judgment. Therefore, he did not stop with asking them for written reports; on a great number of hard problems that came up as the new government was taking shape, he called them together and talked the matter over with them and sometimes with the Vice-President, John Adams, as well. Thus from the very first day there was a Cabinet, in spite of congressional objections, although it was several years before it began to be so called in public. As far as we know, the first person to call these assistants the Cabinet was James Madison, in an article published in 1793 when Washington had already been President for four years. Moreover, it was not until 1907 that any law referred to it by name. By that time the British Cabinet had long since been the highly respected governing committee of the House of Commons that it is today, and its once evil meaning had been forgotten.

Washington paid no attention to those who foretold the dreadful things that a Cabinet would do to the country. He simply determined to get the best man he could to manage each of the departments. Jay had been handling foreign affairs under the old government, and the President first thought of making him Secretary of State. But Jay, who was also a wise man, preferred to be a judge, so Washington made him Chief Justice of the Supreme Court. Washington then turned to Jefferson, who was really better fitted for the job than Jay.

Robert Morris had handled the finances of the old government with great success, if you consider how little he had to work with. Washington naturally thought of him for Secretary of the Treasury. But Morris was a tired man, and his own business needed his attention. Therefore, he suggested a man whom Washington knew very well as an aide-de-camp, but whom he seems not to have thought of as a financier. This man was Alexander Hamilton who, said Morris, knew more than Morris did about handling money. Washington took this advice and Hamilton was appointed.

Knox was the one holdover from the old government. He continued to handle military affairs with the new title of Secretary of War. He had been Washington's chief of artillery, and a good one; but he was all soldier and attended strictly to his own business.

Randolph, the Attorney General, was the least satisfactory of the group, but he wasn't expected to do much about organizing the government.

Thomas Jefferson and Alexander Hamilton were the stars of Washington's Cabinet. At the same time they were the burden of Washington's life. Most history books say little about the trouble they caused him, because so many people think that to admit that a man has great faults is to deny that he is a great man. But every man has faults, and in a great man they are more than likely to be great faults.

Another fact that at first is hard to believe is that often a great man's virtues rather than his faults are what make him troublesome. It is likely that Washington had more cause to worry about the strength than about the weakness of both his Secretary of State and his Secretary of the Treasury. For they were both great men. There is no doubt about that. Both did fine work and deserve much

credit for getting the new nation going. There is no doubt about that, either.

But strong men are always hardheaded men, and so were Hamilton and Jefferson. They held different ideas of what this country ought to be, and each was determined to do all he could to make his idea prevail. Each found the other in his way and tried to push him aside. Soon they were hating each other, and Washington was caught in the middle. Proof that Washington was a greater man than either is the fact that he could handle them both and make them work together. Possibly no other man then living in America could have done so.

Washington wasn't as clever as either of them. He was not nearly as good a speaker as Hamilton, or as good a writer as Jefferson. He was not witty or graceful. He was not even very well educated. But there was something about that man that no other President has had to the same degree. This quality was a strong sense of duty combined with equally strong common sense. Although he wasn't very brilliant or very learned, George Washington was just more of a man than any other American of his time. Both Jefferson and Hamilton knew it, so they worked for him as for no one else.

For the country at that time this combination of men was the best thing that could have happened. Washington's Cabinet was unlike any other in that it was trying a new idea in government and had no model to follow. It had to decide, and then to persuade Washington, not only how the departments should work, but at what they should work— that is, what they should try to do. The job of later Cabinets was mainly to carry on what the first one started; so Washington required of his department heads more than assistance. He needed ideas and in supplying them his Cabinet became more than a group of superintendents, it became a real council of state.

The country had to find its way between two dangers—that of slipping back into tyranny, and that of plunging forward into anarchy. If the new country had been governed by Jefferson alone, it might have plunged forward too fast. If it had been governed by Hamilton alone, it would almost certainly have slipped back into monarchy and probably into tyranny. But it had both Jefferson and Hamilton, and these two strong men were checked by the steadiest man in America.

But the contest between the two showed right at the start that one of a President's hardest tasks is to hold his Cabinet together after he gets it. Some Presidents couldn't do it, and the country got into trouble because of their failure. Not even Washington could hold his Cabinet together through two terms. By the time he had been President for six years only Knox was left of the original four, and Knox had never had any ideas outside of his own department.

The problems on which Hamilton and Jefferson disagreed were all settled long ago, so they are not of much interest now. But the way in which they fought is highly interesting, because Cabinet members are fighting in the same way nearly two hundred years later, and no doubt will continue to fight in the same way as far as we can see into the future.

Hamilton said frankly that he considered the British form of government the best on earth, so he wanted to make ours as much like the British as he could. Jefferson was equally sure that if we didn't invent a better system than the British we couldn't last long, so he favored making our system as different from the British as he could.

It was one of those quarrels in which there were right and wrong on both sides, and the most completely wrong idea was held by both men. Each thought the other would gladly destroy the country to serve his own glory, and in that they were wrong. Yet it is possible to see how they came to this belief. Each had the idea that the other was blocking his efforts, and in that they were right. Each had the idea that the other was interfering in things that, strictly speaking, were none of his business, and in that, too, both were right. Each believed that the other was acting in a sneaky way, and there, again, they were sometimes right. Jefferson, especially in the early days, paid more attention to the noble words of the French Revolutionists than to their bloody deeds, which was bad judgment. Hamilton, we have learned only recently, gave a British agent state secrets that he had no right to give, which was very bad conduct. But when Jefferson believed that Hamilton was knowingly and willfully working for the British king, and Hamilton believed that Jefferson was working for the French dictator, they were utterly wrong.

Each had a group of friends in Congress and each used those friends to block the other's plans. Money problems were Hamilton's business, but when he wanted to take over the war debts of the various states and make them one big debt of the

United States, Jefferson interfered through his friends in Congress and held up the plan until Hamilton agreed to persuade *his* friends to vote for locating the national capital on the Potomac River. Foreign affairs were Jefferson's business, but when he tried to force the British out of the forts they still held on American territory, Hamilton told a British agent that we didn't really intend to fight, so of course they refused to budge.

However, the two did a great deal more than stir up trouble. Hamilton straightened out the country's money matters with great skill; Jefferson made the State Department a smooth-running foreign office that other nations had to respect. By far the most important thing they did, though, was help Washington convince both Americans and foreigners that this new government could really govern.

In the twentieth century the vast power of the United States makes it hard for us to realize that at the end of the eighteenth century many, perhaps most, Americans and nearly all foreigners fully expected the new nation to fall. But in the two terms that Washington served as President, and especially in the first term when the foundations were laid, a government was established under which free men could both rule and protect themselves.

Looking back, we can see that it took all three men to do it. Washington did not have the genius of either of his two great secretaries, but he had the power to control them, because he alone was completely trusted by all the people. Some Americans could, and did, believe that Jefferson was a fool, and others that Hamilton was a crook; but nobody doubted that George Washington was both sane and honest. Thus when he backed a scheme of either Jefferson or Hamilton, the people took his word for it. For this reason the men of genius were able to do their work.

Just before he retired at the end of his second term President Washington issued a statement, since known as the Farewell Address, in which he gave the people his advice about the future conduct of their government. It was good advice, so good that most Presidents have followed it, and all have pretended to follow it for nearly two hundred years. But one part of it has been frequently misunderstood. Washington issued a stern warning against the danger of what he called factions. He predicted that if they were allowed to develop the country would destroy itself, so he earnestly begged the people always to be on guard against factions.

It is often said that by factions Washington meant parties, but there is no reason for saying so. In the first place, at that time the major parties were just beginning to take shape, and Washington was not the man to warn against something that didn't exist. In the second place, Washington always said what he thought, and when he wrote *faction* he meant *faction,* that is, a group blindly devoted to one man or to one idea. Now we call such groups by another name, splinter parties, meaning groups that have split off from one of the major parties like splinters off a board. Factions were, in fact, gathering around Jefferson and Hamilton. Each had a certain number of followers who were more interested in the success of the leader than they were in the good of the country.

Washington was right about the danger of letting fanatics take charge of public affairs, but he was not altogether right. He had already proved it himself by gradually drifting into one faction, that of Hamilton. Washington was as far from being a fanatic as any man could be, but he could not avoid joining a faction to some extent, because the whole country was dividing, apparently into Jeffersonians and Hamiltonians, but really into those who put liberty ahead of law, and those who put law ahead of liberty.

By 1793 Washington felt that American liberty was reasonably safe and that it was time to pay more attention to law and order than Jefferson was inclined to do. So in that year he accepted Jefferson's resignation and made Edmund Randolph Secretary of State. But Randolph was no match for Hamilton, and in a few months the Secretary of the Treasury was running the State Department as well as his own. When the time came to negotiate a commercial treaty with Great Britain, Hamilton insisted that his friend John Jay be sent to represent the United States and privately gave Jay instructions contradicting those given him by Randolph and Washington. Jay came back with a treaty so bad that popular opinion was furious and even Washington's reputation suffered.

Washington knew that someone had given away his plans to get a good treaty from Great Britain, but he didn't know that it was his trusted adviser, Hamilton. Nobody else knew it until many years later, when historians examined the letters and papers of the man who had been the British governor of Canada at that time. Then it was revealed that the governor's agent at Washington had been getting inside information from the American Secretary of the Treasury.

Such an act today would be looked on as a shocking crime, the very next thing to treason. It would not have been taken so seriously in 1793, but even then it would not have been approved, and Hamilton took good care to conceal what he was doing. Probably he did not himself realize that he was betraying Washington; it may be that he thought he was saving Washington from being misled by the hated Jefferson. Yet while we cannot call him a traitor, the facts show that he fancied himself wiser than Washington and Jefferson combined, and that vanity did serious damage to the country.

The President never knew how far Hamilton had gone, but he did know that foreign affairs were being bungled and suspected that Hamilton had something to do with it. So he forced Randolph to quit and, a short time later, accepted Hamilton's resignation. He made Timothy Pickering Secretary of State and Oliver Wolcott Secretary of the Treasury. Both were followers of Hamilton, however, so the administration was entirely made up of Hamiltonians, who were now beginning to call themselves Federalists.

Getting rid of both Jefferson and Hamilton had not caused the parties to disappear, for by this time the moderate men, as well as the fanatics, were beginning to see that the difference between the two men was really between two points of view and that every thinking man must take one or the other. For instance, John Adams, who hated Hamilton, became a Federalist, while James Madison, who had worked in the friendliest way with Hamilton in writing *The Federalist,* became one of the strong leaders of the Jeffersonians, who now called themselves Republicans.

During Washington's second term (1793 to 1797) Jefferson became known as the chief spokesman of the liberal philosophy, which feels that we have much to gain and little to lose by constantly trying out new ways to improve our system. Hamilton became the leader of the conservative, which feels that it is hard to recover from mistakes made in the past and that we have much to lose and little to gain by monkeying around with new ideas. It seems that Washington never clearly understood this division. He feared that people were gathering around Hamilton and Jefferson merely because they liked the men. If this had been true, it would have meant the rise of faction, the thing that he dreaded. But it was not true. Some men who cared little for the leader, and some who definitely hated him, joined his party because they liked its philosophy, whatever they may have thought of the man.

Even Washington saw the trend in at least one of its aspects, that of the makeup of the Cabinet. In 1795, after both Jefferson and Hamilton were out, he said that he would never, knowingly, bring into the Cabinet a man who opposed the general policy of the government, for to do so "would be a sort of political suicide." By the time the second President was elected it was agreed that the members of the Cabinet must be men whose political ideas were, in general, the same as the President's, which is to say, the Cabinet member must belong to the President's party.

JEFFERSON'S TWO RULES

By 1796 Washington had had enough and more than enough. Of the preceding twenty-one years he had spent eight in command of the army, two more in getting the Constitution written and ratified, and eight as President—eighteen years in public service of one kind or another. He had paid next to no attention to his own business. If his wife, Martha, had not been a good manager, he would have lost everything that he had; and he did lose a great deal.

Yet that was only his second reason for refusing to be elected again in 1796. His first was that he was tired—as the common saying is, "tired to death"—of trying to solve the swarm of problems that the President has to face every day. He was disgusted by the way that men in high offices, who should have been thinking of nothing but the country's good, let themselves be turned away from their duty by their greed, or their vanity, or their spite against some rival.

When it became known that Washington would not accept a third term, rivalry broke out immediately, for there was no other man on whom the country could unite. Hamilton was the logical candidate of the Federalists, but he had too many enemies in his own party, so they turned to their second greatest leader, John Adams. With the encouragement of Washington, they decided to vote for him while the Republicans voted for Jefferson. The electoral vote turned out 71 to 68 in favor of Adams; in those days nobody troubled to count the popular vote. At that time the runner-up in the electoral vote, who was Jefferson, became the Vice-President. It had been Washington's idea that if an emergency arose in the absence of the President, the Vice-President should call the Cabinet together to decide what should be done. In 1791, being then at Mount Vernon, he wrote the secretaries that if the Vice-President also should be away when anything happened, they should meet without him, implying that if the Vice-President

should be in town, he would be the one to call the
meeting.

This procedure was all very well when Washington was President and Adams Vice-President,
for their ideas of which way the government
should go were pretty much the same. But it
wouldn't do at all when Adams was President and
Jefferson Vice-President, for their ideas were opposed. So Jefferson announced publicly that he did
not consider himself a member of the Cabinet and
would not attend its meetings.

Jefferson made the excuse that since he presided
over the Senate, and the Senate was part of the
legislative branch, he ought to stay out of the executive branch altogether. The excuse was somewhat weak, for although he presided over the Senate he wasn't a Senator and had no vote except in
case of a tie. His real reason was stronger. He could
see no good in constantly quarreling with Adams's
advisers, which he would certainly do if he attended Cabinet meetings.

If Adams knew that Hamilton had put Pickering
and Wolcott in Washington's Cabinet, he did not
pay enough attention to the fact, for he kept them
in his own Cabinet. But Pickering and Wolcott
knew to whom they owed their jobs and acted ac-

cordingly. Hamilton never denied that Washington was his chief, so his men were loyal to President Washington as the superchief. But when
Washington was gone they regarded Hamilton,
and nobody else, as their chief and took his orders,
although Adams was President.

The fact that John Adams never imagined they
would do any such thing shows that, although he
was a great man when he was dealing with ideas,
he didn't know much about dealing with people.
In other words, he was a great statesman, but a
poor politician, for every politician knows better
than to rely on a man who owes his job to someone
else. From the very start Pickering and Wolcott,
and to a lesser extent McHenry, Secretary of War,
listened more carefully to Hamilton than they did
to Adams, and constant trouble resulted.

Jefferson and his friends knew what was going
on, and while they had no special liking for Adams,
they regarded it as dirty work on Hamilton's part.
So indeed it was; but it doesn't prove that Hamilton was, as they said, trying to knock down the
republic and put us back under a king.

One must remember that at this time the parties
were just taking shape, and nobody clearly understood what they ought to be or would become.

It is plain that Hamilton thought of factions as Washington did. We know that he helped write the Farewell Address, and it is likely that the section on factions was more his idea than Washington's. At any rate, it is clear that he thought of the Federalists as a one-man party and that he was the man, not Adams.

Of course, that doesn't excuse him for constantly interfering with Adams's plans, but it does acquit him of the worst that the Jeffersonians were thinking. Hamilton was not trying to destroy the country. He was trying to save it from Jefferson who, he felt sure, *was* trying to destroy it by leading it after the French into a new revolution.

Hamilton's fault was not treason, it was vanity. He was so sure that he knew better than everybody else that he did things that would have shocked a less conceited man. After all Adams, whatever his faults, was President of the United States, responsible for its safety both from kings abroad and from criminals at home. He needed all the help he could get. Above all, he was entitled to the help of those who thought very much as he did and who constituted the Federalist party.

But Hamilton couldn't see it that way. He thought that *he* was entitled to Adams's support and that the President should carry out the policy that Hamilton thought was wise. The crisis came in 1798, when affairs in Europe were very bad, and Adams was making every effort to keep us out of the mess. He was having a hard time, because nobody in Europe was in a mood to be reasonable, and this country was too weak, too small, and too far away for any European power to be afraid of it.

If Adams's problem had been to dodge between the two great monarchs, the king of England and the king of France, he would have had trouble enough. But it wasn't that simple. In 1798 Napoleon was just rising to power in France. The man Adams had to deal with was the very able but very tricky Talleyrand, French minister of foreign affairs, who made the mistake of insulting the American commissioners by demanding that we make all kinds of concessions and in addition pay him a bribe of $240,000.

Hamilton had always believed that this country's one hope was to make an alliance with England, and when he couldn't persuade Washington and Jefferson, he went behind their back to deal with the British on his own. Now it seemed to him that he had been proved right, and he was all for going to war on the British side. Talleyrand's insolence had made the people very angry, and for once Hamilton seemed to have popular opinion with him.

Preparations for war were begun, and the navies of the two countries didn't wait for orders. Whenever an American and a French ship met a fight started. The Americans, however, proved to be better at sea fighting than any Europeans had expected. We lost a ship or two, but the French lost more, and Talleyrand suddenly realized that this nation, which he had so carelessly slapped in the face, was capable of giving him a very nasty little naval war, which he could not afford at that time.

So he hastily backtracked. He informed President Adams that if the United States would send a new minister to France, he would be received with all respect and anything he said would be carefully considered.

In this country the war party cried, "Oh, no, our national honor has been insulted and the French must not be allowed to get away with it." But what they really meant was that peace with France would spoil the grand scheme of a tie-up with England, and Hamilton, if not the others, honestly believed that this country could not last long without the protection of England.

But John Adams did not see it that way. He believed that it is the first duty of a statesman to keep his country out of war if it is possible to do so without crippling losses. Furthermore, he had spent three years in London as the envoy of the old government. There he had to contend with the king's ministers, and he came away convinced that he could rely on them no more than on the French. He was dead against a tie-up with either side, so when Talleyrand invited him to send a new minister to Paris he sent one promptly.

At this point Hamilton lost his head completely and did something that hurt his reputation worse than anything else. With the help of Pickering and especially of Wolcott, both members of Adams's Cabinet, he wrote and published a furious attack on the President of his country, and set about to secure his defeat in the election of 1800.

At last John Adams waked up to the fact that he had been sold out. He discharged Pickering, Wolcott, and McHenry, but it was too late. The still only half-formed Federalist party was shattered beyond repair, and it never elected another President. When one wing of it deserted Adams, it ceased to be a major party and became a splinter.

But the Federalists had some important effects

on the President's Cabinet. For one thing, in the excitement of 1789 it became plain that one man ought not to try to handle both the Army and the Navy. So a new department was set up, and the Secretary of the Navy joined the Cabinet.

For another, every strong President since Adams has chosen his own Cabinet, trying to select men with whom he can agree and who can be relied on to carry out his policies. The only important exceptions to this rule have occurred when a President has died in office; in such cases the Vice-President has usually taken over the Cabinet with the office. If he makes changes, they will be one at a time.

In 1800 the electors voted under the old rule, by which each of them named two men. The one who got a majority of the votes became President, the next highest became Vice-President. The well-drilled Jeffersonians all voted for the same two men, so the vote came out Thomas Jefferson 73, Aaron Burr 73, John Adams 65, Charles Pinckney 64, John Jay 1. Since the first two men were tied, there was no election. That threw the choice between Jefferson and Burr into the House of Representatives, where each state had one vote. As there were then sixteen states, nine would elect the President. If the Hamilton party could get nine to vote for Burr instead of Jefferson, they would have a wonderful chance to keep the hated Jefferson out of the Presidency, in spite of the fact that the country had voted for him. Everyone knew that the intention had been to make Jefferson President and Burr Vice-President, but that wasn't the way the vote had come out.

This situation put Hamilton on the spot. He hated Jefferson, but he despised Burr, who came from his own state of New York and had played dirty politics against Hamilton there. Yet he would have to support one, and, as he saw it, his choice was not between a crook and an honest man, but between a smart crook and a cheap crook. He decided that the country on the whole would be better off under the man with brains so, doubtless with a heavy heart, he worked for and secured the election of Jefferson. In 1804 this tangle was corrected by the Twelfth Amendment providing that electors should say which man they wanted for President and which for Vice-President. But two years later, in 1806, Burr killed Hamilton in a duel, and there is little doubt that part of the reason for that duel was Burr's hatred of Hamilton for what he had done in this election.

Be that as it may, when Hamilton helped make his greatest enemy President he wiped out all suspicion that he wished to make an end of the republic. If that had been his desire he would have supported Burr, as many of his more reckless followers did. In time Jefferson came to understand this. Years later he decorated the hall of his famous house, Monticello, with likenesses of great men he had known, and we may be sure that none he considered a traitor went into that group. On one side of the hall was a portrait bust of George Washington and on the other side one of Alexander Hamilton.

John Adams seems to have been one of those unlucky persons who have to learn everything the hard way. He was honest, brave, and intelligent, but he just couldn't help getting on other people's nerves. As a result, someone was always hitting him from behind. The worst blow came when he was President and his own party turned on him. He never got the credit that he deserved, and he was an unhappy man.

Thomas Jefferson, on the other hand, had the knack of learning from other people's mistakes. As Vice-President he had been close by when Adams was having his troubles, and Jefferson did not fail to take note. So when he became President he put at the head of the Department of State the best political friend he had, James Madison, and at the head of the Treasury Albert Gallatin, a man who knew more about handling money than even Hamilton, and who was also known for his loyalty to his friends. He made Henry Dearborn Secretary of War, Robert Smith Secretary of the Navy, and Levi Lincoln Attorney General. All these men stayed with him throughout his eight years in the White House except Lincoln, who resigned after three years to go into Massachusetts politics. He was succeeded as Attorney General by John Breckinridge, who died in office and was followed by Caesar Rodney.

By choosing men whom he could trust Jefferson avoided being stabbed in the back, but he did more. The other members of the Cabinet were at best merely competent, but Madison and Gallatin were two of the ablest men in American politics at that time, and the departments of State and Treasury were well run. Jefferson knew it, and he established the rule that has been followed by all wise Presidents since: if you are lucky enough to get a good man, let him run his department without interference from anybody.

It was fairly easy to protect Madison, for it is not often that a politician can gain anything by bothering the Secretary of State, but Gallatin was another matter. For one thing, most people are slow to claim that they know much about diplomacy, but everybody claims to know something, and many think they know everything, about money. For another thing, the Constitution makers had provided that the Secretary of the Treasury must report to the Congress as well as to the President, and this requirement gave rise to the notion that the Secretary of the Treasury somehow belonged to the Congress rather than to the President. Hamilton, for one, held this idea strongly.

Thus Gallatin was constantly under fire. Some of the criticism was open and honest, coming from men who sincerely believed he was making mistakes. These complaints he could meet himself, without any help from the President, and he took them as part of the day's work. But Gallatin was attacked by others who were neither open nor honest. As a youth he had come to this country from Switzerland, and there were some who believed, or pretended to believe, that nobody born abroad is to be trusted. He was an aristocrat, yet he stood up for the poor farmers in the mountains of Pennsylvania. He was highly educated, which made the ignorant suspect him. They told all kinds of wicked lies about him.

Against that sort of thing Gallatin could do nothing for himself, and the friendship of President Jefferson, and later of President Madison, really helped. They knew their man and had nothing but scorn for the lies that were told him. So Gallatin served in all thirteen years as Secretary of the Treasury—longer than any other man, and, as some believe, better than any other man that ever held the office.

The two rules that the third President Jefferson established—first, pick your own men, and, second, when you have found a good one, let him run his department and defend him against anyone who tries to interfere—are good rules, as everyone agrees. The trouble is that they are hard rules to keep, and only a strong President can do so.

CONGRESS REVOLTS

It is possible that Madison knew more about the theory of government than any other man alive in 1808, the year that he was elected. But the theory of government is one thing, and the art of governing is something very different. This fact is one that philosophers have seldom understood.

Madison, as one of the most important among the makers of the Constitution, and as the writer of a large part of *The Federalist,* had proved that he was a philosopher. He had been, also, an excellent Secretary of State under President Jefferson. But when he became President himself he let things get out of hand right from the start, showing that the art of governing was something he did not know.

Madison wanted Gallatin for his Secretary of State. In theory, the idea was fine, for Gallatin had proved that he was honest, reliable, and knew how to run a big department. Later he was to prove that he was also a first-rate diplomatic agent. In theory, he was the perfect man for the job.

But Gallatin still had enemies. Among them were three powerful Senators, Samuel Smith, of Maryland, William Branch Giles, of Virginia, and Michael Leib, of Pennsylvania. All three were notorious demagogues and rarely were they true to any leader of any party.

Madison knew these things, and if he had understood the art of governing he would have realized that he must then and there call for a showdown. If he did not make clear to that trio right at the start that he proposed to be master of the executive branch, they would never give him any peace.

But he gave way. Instead of Gallatin, he made an appointment so bad that it is hard to believe. He named Robert Smith, whom Jefferson had practically thrown out of his Cabinet for sheer incompetence and whose only claim to office was that he was a brother of the powerful Senator Smith. Thus, Madison violated both of Jefferson's rules; he let others choose his Cabinet, and he did not stand behind the good man that he had. Of course, it didn't work. Later Robert Smith had to be kicked out, and Samuel Smith split the party as Madison had been trying to avoid.

Why, then, did Madison do it? The easy explanation that the President's enemies adopted was plain cowardice. But later, in much more dangerous crises, Madison proved that he was brave enough. Another guess, and probably the best one, is that Madison was too much the theorist and too little the practical man. He had seen how the arrogant Hamilton had shattered the Federalist party, while Jefferson, apparently mild-mannered and easygoing, had made the Republican party solid and strong. Without doubt he feared that a knock-down-and-drag-out fight right at the beginning of his term would do for the Republican party what Hamilton had done for the Federalist.

His error was in overlooking the all-important fact that Hamilton was not President. The President has a right, because the people have given him the right, to act like the centurion in the Bible, who could "say to one go, and he goeth, and to another come, and he cometh." What would be arrogance in a mere party leader, such as Hamilton was, is proper firmness in a President. True, his authority is limited to his own executive branch; he cannot give orders to Congress or to the Supreme Court. But the Cabinet is part of the executive; it is the President's, not the party's, Cabinet, and if he doesn't control it, it will run wild.

In eight years Madison had two Secretaries of State, four Secretaries of the Treasury, four Secretaries of War, and three Secretaries of the Navy, not to mention three Attorneys General, although that post was not yet considered a Cabinet office. Such a merry-go-round is more than a hint that nobody in the Cabinet knew quite where he was or exactly what he was expected to do. That is to say, nobody was boss.

Madison did have one excuse. The time was rough in any country for statesmen who wanted to be reasonable. The French had conceived in 1789 a new idea of what government should be like, and they were trying to force that idea upon the rest of the world. This effort lasted twenty-six years with almost incessant war until Napoleon was finally defeated in 1815. Madison's Presidency came in the last third of the period. Washington, Adams, and Jefferson had all faced the same situation, yet had managed somehow to keep things in hand. Madison failed, and his failure cannot be blamed entirely on the world situation. He simply was not masterful enough to cow his enemies.

If they had all been like the three Senators, perhaps he could have brought them to heel. Smith, Giles, and Leib might be the political bosses of Maryland, Virginia, and Pennsylvania, but the rest of the country had little enthusiasm for them. Plainly they were out for what they could get for themselves.

But another group of a different kind also rose against Madison. They were young members of Congress who had been children during the Revolution. Two of the ablest, in fact, were not born until after Cornwallis surrendered at Yorktown. These men knew war only by hearsay; they had never been through a campaign. Many of them were from what was then the far West, the country between the Appalachians and the Mississippi River. The West was a country of young men, for the middle-aged and elderly seldom pushed beyond the mountains.

They came to Washington angry over the way the country seemed to be kicked about like a football between France and England. In the combat of the giants every neutral nation was being treated the same way, but that meant nothing to the angry young men. All that mattered to them was that the United States was being slapped around, now by France, now by England, occasionally by both. The War Hawks, as they were called, had nothing in particular against Madison as a man, but as a President they considered him pretty poor stuff, weak-kneed and wobbly, and they were determined to make him stand up against any country that insulted the flag.

This policy was foolish, because we simply did not have the ships, the men, or the weapons required to fight a first-class power. We got away with it after 1776 only because France—for her own purposes, of course—not only supplied us with weapons and money, but actually sent a strong fleet and a stronger army to help. There was no chance of such help in Madison's time, and he knew it.

But the War Hawks had the ear of the public. After all, while they might have been foolish, they were not chisellers and grafters. They talked about honor, not about profit, and it sounded fine to a great many Americans, much finer than the President's warning to be cautious. Madison could make no headway against them, and they drove him steadily toward war. Many of them did not care whether he fought France or England, but fight somebody he must.

Plainly Congress was making an effort to take the conduct of foreign affairs out of the hands of the President and his agent, the Secretary of State. The two most brilliant leaders of the War Hawks were Henry Clay, of Kentucky, and John C. Calhoun, of South Carolina. In later years each of these men was to be Secretary of State, and each became indignant when members of Congress tried to tell them how to run the department.

But now they were on the other side of the fence, and it was they, rather than such cheap-Jacks as Smith, Giles, and Leib, who drove Madison into a war that we were not prepared to fight. This war, the War of 1812, resulted in the surrender of an American army at Detroit, the capture and burning of Washington, a scandalous defeat at Niagara, and an effort by New England Federalists to secede—an effort, by the way, that finished the Federalists even as a splinter party.

Eventually Madison dealt with the Senatorial conspirators successfully if in a rather undignified way. After about a year in office he got proof of what he had been unwilling to believe—that Rob-

ert Smith, his Secretary of State, was conspiring against him with the three Senators. Madison called the man into his office and denounced him to his face in bitter terms. The story in Washington was that the quarrel became so heated that Smith lost his head completely and actually struck at the President of the United States with his cane. Madison is said to have snatched up the tongs from the fireplace to defend himself before an attendant rushed between them.

That fight has never been proved and is perhaps just Washington gossip. But it is a known fact that the interview was a hot one, and it is a known fact that Smith was not merely asked to resign, he was dismissed, fired from his job without any polite letter of regrets or any kind of apology. Madison then did what he should have done in the first place; he appointed a man on whom he could rely, James Monroe, and had no more trouble with the State Department.

This struggle was the first great effort by Congress to make the Cabinet subservient to it rather than to the President. The curious thing is that James Madison himself, in the essays he wrote for *The Federalist,* especially in Number Ten of that series, had pointed out that it was to be expected that each of the three branches of government would try to take over the other two. He also expected the others to resist successfully any such effort. Yet he was not prepared for what he himself had predicted. When the three Senators were pushing Robert Smith on him, he did *not* resist successfully. To that extent he deserved the embarrassment that followed.

AN ABLE SECRETARY OF STATE

The election of the fifth President, James Monroe, in 1816 marked the start of a period that has come to be known as the Era of Good Feeling, meaning that there were no party battles in the eight years that Monroe was in the White House. The reason was that there was no party to do battle with the Republicans, not even a one-man or one-idea splinter party.

Yet if there were no party battles, there was plenty of fighting inside what was now beginning to be called the Democratic-Republican party. This development was not surprising, for everybody was in the one party, even the son of that stoutest of Federalists, John Adams. Some historians have said that, far from being an era of good feeling, it was an era of more vicious ill-feeling than almost any other in our history.

Nevertheless, Monroe was able to appoint a relatively quiet Cabinet. It is best for a President to be wise, but the next best thing is for him to be able to know wisdom when he sees it in other men. Monroe showed this ability by the selection of his Cabinet. For Secretary of State he chose John Quincy Adams, son of John Adams, who had been taken along by his father on several diplomatic missions, had himself been minister to Russia, and had helped write the peace treaty after the War of 1812; which is to say, he really knew foreign relations.

As Secretary of the Treasury Monroe kept the man that Madison had appointed near the end of his second term, William H. Crawford, a good enough financier and a first-rate politician.

As Secretary of War he chose one of the young War Hawks, John C. Calhoun, a bit slippery and hard to manage, but a man with great energy and with one of the finest minds in the country.

To the post of Attorney General Monroe appointed William Wirt, without doubt one of the best lawyers in the country and a dependable friend.

To the Navy Department Monroe sent Smith Thompson, whom he later put on the Supreme Court, and in his place put Samuel L. Southard. Neither of these men did distinguished work, but at least they did not try to sell out their chief.

However, in Adams, Crawford, Calhoun, and Wirt, Monroe had four strong men, and such men are hard to manage. The best thing to be said for Monroe is that he was able to drive such a four-horse team without upsetting the wagon. Each of the four felt perfectly capable of being President himself. Probably each felt that he would make a better President than Monroe. Yet somehow he managed to keep them in line, a remarkable feat in view of their characters. Adams was prickly, ir-ritable, suspicious, and capable of poisonous hatred. Crawford was ambitious, pompous, and a masterly wheeler and dealer in politics. Calhoun was even more ambitious, proud, and so sure of his infallibility that he was often stubbornly wrong. Wirt was probably the most likable of the four, but a stickler for the letter of the law and inclined to believe that others had no proper respect for it.

Yet each was a man of great ability in his own line, and with them Monroe proved that a Presi-dent whose own mind is not of the first rank can yet, with a good Cabinet and the skill to manage it, make a surprisingly good record.

The Cabinet came to Monroe's rescue in 1820, the year that he came up for reelection. In August Congress handed the President a very hot potato in what was known as the Missouri Compromise. There were then twenty-two states in the Union, eleven slave and eleven free, which made the balance even in the Senate. The North, having more people, had more Representatives, so the South was determined to keep the balance in the Senate. Then Maine and Missouri applied for admission. There was no doubt that Maine would be a free state; the question was as to Missouri. Could Congress admit it on condition that it should be a slave state, to balance Maine? Whether it had a right to do so or not, it did.

Everyone knew that the slavery question was political dynamite, and thus far Congress had managed to avoid touching it, but now it had to be faced. When news came to Thomas Jefferson that a debate on slavery had begun, it alarmed him, he said, "like a fire bell in the night." President Monroe was even more alarmed, for he would have to issue, or refuse to issue, the proclamation admitting the new states.

He called the Cabinet together and the discussion was long and anxious. Everyone agreed that the right of Congress to legislate on slavery within a state was doubtful. But it had done so, and the question before the Cabinet was, should the President sign his name to a proclamation that he feared was unconstitutional? In the end they decided that he had better go along with Congress, even if he was taking a chance. So he did, and the country calmed down, postponing the Civil War for forty years.

Possibly this act also saved the Union, for during these forty years the North steadily gained strength, and the South as steadily lost strength. Yet when the break did come, the North won only after four years of desperate fighting.

James Monroe has never been listed among the great Presidents, yet he was so successful that when he came up for reelection in 1820 he carried every state in the Union and received every electoral vote but one. An elector from New Hampshire cast his vote for John Quincy Adams. He said he did so, because he could not bear to have any man except George Washington get every electoral vote, but his neighbors said he acted from pure contrariness. Anyhow, Monroe clearly satisfied the country, and a man who can do that must have some uncommon qualities.

His record is the more surprising when one remembers that at this time public affairs, at home and abroad, were moving with such speed that politicians and statesmen were made dizzy trying to keep up with them. Napoleon was finally beaten down, just before Monroe became President, but he had wrecked Europe completely.

At such times of upheaval all kinds of wild schemes are taken seriously and some actually tried. At this time a particularly wild one was put together by the czar of Russia, the emperor of Austria, and the king of Prussia under the most unsuitable name of the Holy Alliance. It was an alliance all right, but it was far from holy; it was an attempt to put together again the old tyrannies that the French Revolution had broken to pieces.

This alliance looked dangerous to the United States. Spain was having more and more trouble holding down her colonies, from Mexico to the other end of South America, and the king of Spain was hoping to get the Holy Alliance to help him defeat the Latin-American rebels. Monroe knew that if the combined kings of Europe got control of South America, and especially of Mexico, the

United States would be in for trouble, for they were frank to say that they intended to abolish all republics all over the world.

It was long believed that Adams said to Monroe, but we now think that Monroe said to Adams, that it might be well to stop this business before it really got started. But no matter who had the idea first, the President and the Secretary of State agreed that the Holy Alliance must not get a foothold on this side of the Atlantic. This policy suited the British foreign minister, Canning, for the king of England suspected that the Holy Alliance meant no good to him either. Canning suggested to Adams that the two nations file a joint protest.

But the Secretary of State was the son of old John Adams, and as proudly independent as his father had been. He was glad to know that Canning was friendly, but he thought it would be better for the United States to publish its own determination, which Canning could then back up or not, as he saw fit. So in 1823 in his annual message to Congress—now called the State of the Union Message—James Monroe declared publicly that the United States regarded the Americas, both of them, as no longer suitable places for any European nation to set up colonies. Henceforth, it would regard any attempt to colonize them as an act unfriendly to the United States. In ordinary, not diplomatic, language these words meant, "Stay out, or we fight."

This statement was the famous Monroe Doctrine.

At first the Holy Alliance may have been inclined to laugh, but the thing became serious when Canning let it be known that the British thought the Americans had a pretty good idea. Their attitude put a different face on it. Since the battle of Trafalgar every statesman had known that nobody could hope to transport an army across the Atlantic if the British navy blocked the way. So Spain had to give up hope of help from the Holy Alliance, and alone she could not hold the colonies. Thus, the independence of Latin America began, and the Monroe Doctrine, more than anything else, has kept Monroe's name familiar to Americans of later generations.

Affairs at home, however, were becoming as confused as affairs abroad. The Federalist party was finished, but the people were still divided into those who were all for pushing ahead with our experiment in self-government, and those who thought it more important to hang on to what we had gained, making it stronger and more solid. For both these ways of thinking to be represented by the same party was not possible. It was bound to divide and, after Monroe, it did.

Those who thought it more important to be careful than to be swift, the conservative, were beginning to gather around the brilliant young War Hawk from Kentucky, Henry Clay. As more and more people poured into the Mississippi valley, the West grew more and more important, and its leaders gained more and more influence in Washington. Clay represented, not the explorers and pioneers of the West, but its solid businessmen who, following the pioneers, turned clearings into plantations, and trading posts into towns and cities.

But the West had its daring element, too, its liberals, and they had no liking for Clay, who was, they thought, too friendly to the rich and well-born in the Eastern states. Western liberals preferred the national military hero, Andrew Jackson, a famous Indian fighter and also the only American general of the War of 1812 who had defeated an army of British regulars.

In the East, however, Jackson was regarded doubtfully for the reason that as an Indian fighter

he had been a little too good. Sent against the Seminoles, who had been raiding Georgia from Spanish Florida, Jackson not only threw them out of Georgia, he pursued them into Spanish territory. When the Spanish governor of Pensacola protested, the American locked him in his own jail. On top of that, when Jackson caught a pair of British civilians furnishing arms and information to the Indians, he hanged them both.

Naturally, these acts brought furious protest from Madrid and London. Calhoun, Secretary of War, had never liked Jackson anyhow, and he favored giving the wild general a sharp dressing down, if not a court-martial. But Adams, who also didn't like Jackson, but did like a general who could and would fight, opposed this idea. Since it was Adams, as Secretary of State, who would have to pacify Madrid and London, Calhoun finally followed his lead. Adams, instead of apologizing to the British and Spanish, flung back a long list of countercharges against both, and in the years of wrangling that ensued Jackson's raid was eventually forgotten.

This instance shows what a first-rate Secretary of State can do for a President whom he likes and really wishes to help. Adams saved Monroe from making a bitter enemy of a national hero. Incidentally, Jackson should have become Adams's friend for life, but he didn't, because the truth was concealed. Jackson was given to understand that in a secret Cabinet meeting Adams had tried to have him punished and Calhoun had been the man who saved him.

In this case and throughout the eight years of his terms, Monroe's administration proved that a strong Cabinet, under steady control, can be immensely valuable to a President.

In 1824 every man who amounted to much in national politics looked on himself as a member of the Democratic-Republican party. Even John Quincy Adams, son of the Federalist chief, had turned Democratic-Republican. In that year four of them decided to run for the Presidency. They were Adams and Crawford, both members of Monroe's Cabinet, Clay, recognized leader of the West, and Jackson, who was threatening to take that leadership from Clay. But before election day Crawford, who up to that point had been running well, suffered a paralytic stroke and dropped back, although he did not quit the race. The electoral vote came out: Jackson, 99, Adams, 84, Crawford, 41,

Clay, 37. Since no man had a majority of the electoral votes, there was no election.

This outcome threw the decision into the House of Representatives, and the Twelfth Amendment says that in such a case the House shall choose one of the three highest, which put Clay out.

The Senate, which selects the Vice-President if no candidate gains a majority, had nothing to do. John C. Calhoun, another member of Monroe's Cabinet, had been easily elected to that office.

In the House each of the twenty-five states had one vote. With Clay out, the votes of the states that he had won would elect either Jackson or Adams, for most Representatives believed that Crawford was physically disabled. Clay then faced the decision that Hamilton had faced twenty-four years earlier; he must choose between two rivals.

The voters' choice was plainly Jackson, and Clay would have been wiser to admit the fact and go along with it. But up to this time the voters had usually been content to be guided by the advice of their better-informed leaders, and to Clay that was as it should be. He did not believe, as Jefferson did, that the people were capable of choosing for themselves more wisely than anyone could choose for them. He also failed to recognize that the leaders were pointing four ways at once, so the people had to make a choice. Even if they made a poor one, he would have done better to accept it than to give the appearance of trying to overrule the people. Still, the law said that if the people did not elect a President, the House of Representatives should, so Clay felt free to use his own judgment.

That judgment told him to support Adams, for two reasons. In the first place, he was an able statesman. Clay had known that ever since the time, in 1814, when he had worked with Adams and Gallatin making the peace treaty, at Ghent, that ended the War of 1812. It has been said that those three—the other two American delegates did not count for much—won at the conference table a war that had been lost on the battlefield. Afterward, Adams had been a good minister to Great Britain and a very fine Secretary of State. He seemed to have all that it took to make a good President. Jackson was a first-rate army commander, but what else he might be good for Clay did not know.

He did know, though—and this knowledge gave him his second reason for preferring Adams—that Jackson was immensely popular in the West, which Clay regarded as his own special territory. If Jackson became President he would overshadow Clay where Clay could not afford to be overshadowed. So Clay threw his support to Adams, who was elected.

Up to this point Clay was safe. His first reason for supporting Adams, the man's known ability, was perfectly right and proper. His second reason, not to build up a Western rival, was not so good, yet it was one that most people could understand and not many would blame him for. However, Clay and Adams together then made a bad mistake.

John Quincy Adams, like his father, had a fine mind, complete honesty, and great courage; but he also had his father's worst defect, a lack of understanding of how things look to other men. To John Quincy Adams right was right and wrong was wrong; if the right thing looked wrong to Tom, Dick, or Harry, then no attention should be paid to Tom, Dick, or Harry. The right thing should be done anyhow.

No doubt that reasoning is good morals, but it is bad politics. A good politician can and will explain to those who don't understand why what he is doing is right. The explanation slows him, and sometimes it prevents him from doing anything.

But in the long run it pays, for what he does do is then too solid for his enemies to knock down.

Thomas Jefferson had been Secretary of State and became President. James Madison had been Secretary of State and became President. James Monroe had been Secretary of State and became President. John Quincy Adams had been Secretary of State and became President. Adams thought that a President should make a man Secretary of State because the man can do the job. In this belief he was quite right. A great many people, however, looking at the record, thought that if he made a man Secretary of State it was in the expectation that he would become President. Therefore, they believed that the man Adams made head of the State Department was the man he intended to make President.

Following his convictions, Adams offered to make Clay Secretary of State as soon as he was elected, and Clay accepted. In theory this appointment was quite right, but in practice it was all wrong, the worst thing either of them could have done. What counted was how it looked, and it looked bad. Adams, a poor politician, perhaps couldn't understand this fact, but Clay, one of the best politicians of his time, should have seen it.

They had ample warning. Before the vote was taken in the House, when it became known that Clay might swing to Adams, a great howl went up. Rabid partisans, Crawford's as well as Jackson's, loudly asserted that the whole thing was a frame-up, designed to make Clay President as soon as Adams's term was over, for wasn't the State Department the anteroom to the Presidency? Therefore, Adams had bought and Clay had sold his support. "Bargain and corruption!" was the cry, and neither Adams nor Clay ever got over the damage that it did.

Yet, knowing what people were saying, Clay went along with the proposal. He persuaded himself that to refuse the job would be to admit that there had been a deal. That idea is what he wanted to believe, and a man persuades himself easily to believe what he wants to believe. There had been no deal in so many words; but when he accepted the office he convinced the public that there had been one, if only in understanding.

The mistake was fatal, for thereafter he never had a real chance to become President. He was nominated three times, but always against an unbeatable opponent. When his party did have a chance to win, it turned to another candidate.

The mistake also ruined John Quincy Adams, for in 1828 Adams was defeated by Andrew Jackson. Up to that time he and his father were the only Presidents who had been refused a second term, and there is little doubt that the chief reason for his defeat was the taint of scandal that stuck to his administration ever after the cry of "Bargain and corruption!" was raised. While an able Secretary of State may be the making of a President, as John Quincy Adams was of Monroe, an equally able Secretary may be his undoing, as Henry Clay was of John Quincy Adams.

THE KITCHEN CABINET

Henry Clay's error in accepting the post of Secretary of State under John Quincy Adams was not all that raised Jackson to the Presidency. There was a great deal more to it than that. A change was coming over the country.

In America there were no classes in the eyes of the law, but in the eyes of the people there were two, gentlemen and those described as the common people. In the years right after the Revolution Americans generally agreed that running the government was the business of the gentlemen.

There was a great deal of talk, especially in Fourth of July orations, about democracy and equality, but most of the people thought it was just fancy, pleasant to hear, but not to be taken seriously. So they listened to the speeches, shouted "Hurrah!" and went on leaving the business of government pretty much to the gentlemen.

For a good many years the gentlemen were well acquainted with the people, knew what they needed, and were fairly successful in giving it to them. It was possible for them to govern this way because most of the people did the same kind of work and lived the same kind of life.

But among the people who were pouring across the Appalachians into the Mississippi valley there were few gentlemen in the old sense. The motto of the frontier was, "Every man for himself and devil take the hindmost!" In the old and thickly populated East the well-educated were the natural leaders whom others followed as much out of habit as anything else. But in the West, where Indians were still a threat, where forests had to be cleared away, and where help was always distant and often not to be had, the natural leaders were those who were strongest, boldest, and toughest. Those who were not strong, bold, and tough either went back East or died.

To these people democracy was not a theory, it was a fact. Any man who could stand on his own two feet was quite as good as one whose ancestors had been governors, doctors of divinity, or owners of great plantations. Equality, to them, meant an equal chance to acquire any of the good things that were to be had. They respected a man who could handle ax and plow and especially one who could shoot fast and straight. To names they paid little attention.

Neither the Virginians nor the New Englanders really understood these people. So after the defeat of Adams one group of Congressmen gathered around Clay, another around Jackson, and this division brought back the two-party system.

The Clay men felt that the name Federalist had become rather a dirty word, so they chose another and looked back to England for it. Tory wouldn't do, for in this country the word meant one who had opposed the Revolution, so they settled on Whig, although it was the name of the liberal party in England, and they were conservatives.

In view of the fact that Adams had called himself a Democratic-Republican, Jackson's crowd also wanted a new name. So they called themselves Democrats, without the hyphen. But all the Whigs and many of the Democrats in Congress took it for granted that their function was to make the great decisions and the voters had only to follow.

Up to 1824 parties had chosen their candidate for President, by calling their members into a meeting, known as a caucus, and naming the man of their choice. Then the people were supposed to elect one or the other. This scheme had worked fairly well, but in that year Jackson had not been nominated by a caucus. He had been put into the Presidential race first by the legislature of his own state of Tennessee, then by other groups in other states including many people not in Congress. In 1824 more people voted for him than for any caucus-nominated candidate, and in 1828 they elected him overwhelmingly. His victory finished the caucus system of nominating candidates once and for all.

Every election brings new men to Washington, but that of 1828 brought a new kind of man as well. He thought about politics and government in a way to which Washington was not accustomed and which it did not understand for a long time. Jackson himself was not unknown to Washington. He had served in both the House and the Senate, and, as a former army commander, he was known to a great many officials. But he brought with him to the capital supporters the like of whom Washington had never seen before.

Old-fashioned politicians were appalled, and so were most of the long-time residents of the city who were not officials. The frontiersmen were strong, but they were not handsome, either in their faces or in their manners. The reception at the White House after the inauguration turned into something not far short of a riot. The jam was terrific. Everyone wanted to see the new President, and the men in hobnailed boots climbed on damask-covered chairs and even on polished tables to catch a glimpse of him. The waiters were jostled, drinks were spilled, glasses smashed, and women fainted. The furniture of the White House was almost wrecked until at last someone had the bright idea of setting up tubs of liquor on the lawn, whereupon the crowd poured outside so fast that some went through the windows instead of the doors.

The old-timers asked what else could you expect, now that a wild barbarian had been elected President, and they clung to that idea long after Jackson had proved that he was one of the smartest politicians in the country and a very strong President. Even when Jackson did things that wise men approved, he did them in a way that set foolish gossips to sneering. The fact is that in all his important acts Jackson was careful to respect the law, but he had little respect for lawyers and less for custom and precedent. Because a thing had always been done in a certain way seemed to him no reason at all for continuing to do it that way, if he could think of a better. Such reasoning upsets people who are ruled by habit.

However, although Jackson had beaten Adams by six to five in popular votes, and by more than two to one in electoral votes, his victory had not been won without a great deal of dickering among the politicians. Calhoun, for instance, saw fairly soon that he could not win the Presidency himself, yet there were a good many people who would vote as he told them. So his men got together with Jackson's men, especially a certain Major William B. Lewis, who had won the general's confidence as his quartermaster during the Indian wars, and they made what they called a gentlemen's agreement and other people called a deal. Calhoun was to have the Vice-Presidency and at least one of his friends was to be placed in the Cabinet. Lewis had already won over Senator Martin Van Buren, of New York, on the understanding that Van Buren, too, would have a high office if Jackson won.

Thus Jackson's hands were somewhat tied when he came to select a Cabinet. He had become a strong personal, as well as political, friend of Van Buren and gladly made him Secretary of State. But for political reasons he had to take Ingham, of Pennsylvania, for Secretary of the Treasury, Branch, of North Carolina, for Secretary of the Navy, and Berrien, of Georgia, for Attorney General, although he knew they were not his men. But he made an old friend, Eaton, of Tennessee, Secretary of War. Five days after the inauguration he announced that the Postmaster General should thenceforth be considered a member of the Cabinet and gave the post to Barry, another old friend.

The arrangement was the best he could manage, but it was uneasy from the start. Jackson had no confidence whatever in Ingham, Branch, and Berrien, suspecting that they were more loyal to Calhoun than to him. Jackson was one of the world's fiercest haters, but at this time he did not especially hate Calhoun, he regarded him merely as a political rival. Major Lewis fixed that. By a carefully planned accident he dropped a letter from Crawford, former Secretary of the Treasury, where Jackson would be sure to see it. In this letter Crawford revealed that Calhoun, the then Secretary of War, had wanted to punish Jackson for his Pensacola raid while Adams, then Secretary of State, had stood by the general.

This information changed Jackson's feeling toward Calhoun into a hatred equal to what he felt for Adams and Clay, who, he thought, had stolen the election from him in 1824. The idea of having three of Calhoun's men among his intimate advisers was intolerable, but how could he get rid of them without starting a fight that might split the party? For months he could see no way to do so, and his rage merely smouldered.

But one thing he could do, and that was to beware of taking these men's advice on anything of importance, for he was sure they would advise him to do what was best for Calhoun rather than for him. Yet Jackson was facing some very hard questions to which he had to find answers. If he didn't want everything he said and did promptly reported to his enemy, he couldn't talk them over with the Cabinet. Van Buren was an exception. Jackson did rely on him. But Eaton and Barry, while loyal enough, were no mental giants, and the President needed sound advice; so he began more and more to consult certain men in minor offices.

Major Lewis, for whom Jackson had found a

place in the Treasury Department, was one. Another was Isaac Hill, a New Hampshire editor-politician, to whom Jackson gave another small job. But the anti-Jackson Senate refused to confirm Hill, so he went back to New Hampshire and got himself elected to the very Senate that had rejected him. A third was Amos Kendall, of Kentucky, another editor-politician. It soon became apparent that these men, with Van Buren, had more influence at the White House than did the heads of departments.

They were all men who knew how to keep their mouths shut, and they never appeared in the room where the Cabinet met. The joke makers began to say that while Jackson met his official Cabinet in the front parlor, where everybody could see them, he met his real advisers in the back of the house, out of sight, perhaps in the kitchen.

Thus the famous Kitchen Cabinet, which Jackson's enemies pretended to believe was a terrible thing, came to be. They said it upset the American system, probably was against the Constitution, and showed that Jackson's real desire was to make himself King Andrew the First.

Such men in the background were well-known in countries under one-man rule, but they were supposed to be impossible in a democracy. Sometimes one was called the court favorite, sometimes the power behind the throne, but the most telling description came from the French. It was the Gray Eminence, after an influential monk who wore the gray robe of the Capuchin order, and who advised Cardinal Richelieu.

For a time Major Lewis, more than any other member of the Kitchen Cabinet, played the part of Gray Eminence to Andrew Jackson. In the latter part of the administration Amos Kendall had about as much influence. Neither held an important office, but Jackson had confidence in them and was more likely to listen to them than to half his regular Cabinet. As a result, the power of each was greatly exaggerated, and both were feared and hated.

Because they had little or no official standing, these men were regarded with suspicion, for nobody was sure how influential they were, and rumor exaggerated their power. Gossips said that they led the President by the nose and really ran the government. This charge was not true, but they did have some power and members of the Cabinet knew it. Therefore, they detested the men and did all they could to discredit them.

The Constitution, however, doesn't compel the

President to consult with anyone. He only has to win the consent of the Senate in appointing important officers and in making treaties. If the President seeks advice, he does so of his own accord, and he is free to seek it from anybody. Unless he is extremely foolish, he will try to choose as great officers of state men whose advice is worth having, but nearly always politics forces him to take into the Cabinet some men he would rather not have. Jackson was forced to take in three, and it was good sense on his part not to let them get the idea that they were running the administration.

When he had been in office about two years, however, a way out of the jam was opened, strangely enough, by Eaton, who otherwise had never counted for much. Just before his appointment Eaton, then a widower, married the daughter of a tavern keeper named O'Neale. She was the widow of what is now called a petty officer in the Navy, and there had been scandalous gossip about her goings-on while her husband was at sea. So the wives of the other Cabinet members, and especially Mrs. Calhoun, wife of the Vice-President, refused to have anything to do with her.

Jackson investigated the tales and found no proof whatever that Peggy O'Neale had done any-

thing worse than flirt a bit with the guests in her father's tavern. Jackson was known to be especially sensitive to that kind of slander because his own wife, now dead, had been the victim of vicious lies, so he stood by Peggy. So did Van Buren, who, as a widower, had no wife to worry about. The affair grew and grew, and by 1831 Washington was boiling with gossip.

According to Van Buren, when he and the President were horseback riding one afternoon, he suggested a plan. As Secretary of State he was considered the head of the Cabinet. If the head of the Cabinet resigned, all the other members customarily did so. Van Buren then offered to hand in his resignation, giving some kind of public excuse that nobody would believe. Privately, he would tell his friends that the Eaton mess had grown so bad that he couldn't stand it any longer, and that reason they would believe. In an hour it would be all over Washington that Peggy had blown up the Cabinet. The Calhoun men would be out, but the party would not be split because everybody would think that they had been thrown out on account of Peggy, not because they were Calhoun men.

At first Jackson wouldn't listen, because he wanted to keep Van Buren. But the more he thought about it, the more perfect the scheme seemed to be. So he consented. Van Buren handed in his resignation, and all the rest had to follow suit. The sensation was tremendous. Eaton threatened to shoot Ingham, whose wife had done a great deal of talking about Peggy, and Ingham skipped out of town after dark. Everyone had a different story, but all the stories agreed on the one point that the Eaton affair had wrecked the Cabinet. Years passed before people even suspected that Jackson's chief aim was to clean out the Calhoun men and that Peggy was a convenient excuse.

So Edward Livingston, of New York, became Secretary of State, Louis McLane, of Delaware, Secretary of the Treasury, Lewis Cass, of Ohio, Secretary of War, Levi Woodbury, of New Hampshire, Secretary of the Navy, and Roger B. Taney, of Maryland, Attorney General. Barry alone of the old Cabinet remained as Postmaster General, but nobody paid much attention to that.

All these men were ones that the President felt he could rely on. All did, in fact, stick to him except McLane, who could not agree with him on the question of the Bank of the United States. But McLane's opposition was honest and aboveboard, and Jackson did not resent it.

The Bank of the United States was a useful institution, because it supplied the only kind of money that can be used by a big country doing big business. That money is credit, not coin. But credit is not a thing that one can see, hear, touch, taste, or smell. It is, as we say, intangible. If one man feels that another with whom he deals will do what he promises, that man has credit with him.

But suppose he has never seen him before, how then can he feel sure? National bank notes were one answer. A person turned his gold and silver over to a bank, and the bank gave him printed slips of paper, which were promises that the bank would pay so many dollars in gold or silver to anyone who brought in the slip.

Congress had chartered the Bank of the United States in 1816 for twenty years. In it the government deposited all the money it collected in taxes and other ways. Then the Bank issued its notes, and the government guaranteed that they would be paid. This guarantee made the notes good anywhere in the United States, for everyone knew the government.

So far, so good. The central Bank at Philadelphia set up branches in various cities around the country, and the notes issued by them were convenient money, easy to carry and good everywhere. But the notes were not issued against gold and silver alone; a man might obtain bank notes by giving the Bank a claim on any kind of property. However, the property had to be worth the money, and if the directors decided that it was not, they would not give notes for it.

As a result, the Bank held great power. By refusing a businessman's pledges, it could deprive him of the money necessary to conduct his business. The catch was that while the government was responsible for whatever the Bank of the United States did, it could not control the Bank. It owned only one third of the stock and named only one third of the directors; the rest were private citizens and they could outvote the government men two to one. This power was, as Jackson believed, too much for any group of private citizens to have.

Nicholas Biddle, president of the Bank, was a good banker, but a poor politician. He was fascinated by Henry Clay and made the mistake of letting Clay use the Bank in politics. Several of the branches had tried to make businessmen vote against Jackson in 1828. Naturally Jackson became persuaded that the Bank was trying to rule the country, and he determined to break it.

The Bank's charter ran until 1836, but Jackson was up for reelection in 1832, and Clay meant to run against him. He got the idea that if he could get Jackson entangled with the Bank, the Bank's power would defeat him and elect Clay. So he persuaded Biddle to apply to Congress for a renewal of the charter four years ahead of time.

Congress promptly passed a bill to recharter the Bank, and Jackson as promptly vetoed it. In the veto message he furiously denounced all monopolies, especially a money monopoly, and proclaimed his intention of fighting them.

This reaction was exactly what Clay had expected, and he and Biddle were so delighted that the Bank had 30,000 copies of the message printed and distributed all over the country. Unfortunately for them, the Bank didn't have half as many friends as they thought. Big businessmen were for it, but little businessmen feared and hated it, while workers who had little to do with banks just didn't care.

The outcome was that Jackson was reelected with a whoop. He won larger majorities, both popular and electoral, than he had received in 1828.

Then Clay's idea backfired in a really big way. Up to this time Jackson had been hoping to curb the Bank's power rather than to kill it, and apparently he had not intended to do anything until the charter ran out in 1836. But since it had made open war on him in 1832, he determined to finish it immediately.

There was much to be said in favor of the Bank, especially since Nicholas Biddle had been its president. It had too much power, but Biddle had used that power more often against crooks than against honest businessmen. He had stamped out a great many swindling schemes, and he had given the country a money system that was working well.

Even some of the President's close advisers thought that he was going too far when he decided to kill the Bank. Van Buren, having gone as minister to England, was out of the way, but others, especially Secretary of the Treasury McLane and Major Lewis of the Kitchen Cabinet, preferred something milder. But they were up against Andrew Jackson. He flatly ordered the Treasury to deposit no more money in the Bank of the United States and to pay the government's bills by checks on the Bank until the money already deposited was withdrawn. McLane squirmed out by getting himself transferred to the State Department, and William J. Duane, a Pennsylvanian appointed to succeed McLane, refused to obey the order. Jackson instantly fired him and appointed Roger B. Taney, of Maryland, Secretary of the Treasury. Taney, long an enemy of the Bank, cheerfully obeyed the order.

All these events happened while Congress was not in session, but when it reassembled the uproar was tremendous. Clay and his friends tried to prove that Jackson's acts were illegal, because the Secretary of the Treasury was really an agent of Congress rather than of the President. This fight was the second serious effort of Congress to make the Cabinet responsible to it rather than to the President, but it failed, partly because the Jacksonians had gained votes in the House and partly because some of the anti-Jackson men were doubtful about trying to invade the executive branch.

Thus the Jackson administration established the principle that the President is boss of the Cabinet. If a secretary cannot get along with the President, he should resign. If he will not resign, he should be thrown out and, if the President is strong, he will be.

CONGRESS REVOLTS AGAIN

Martin Van Buren was made the eighth President by his enemies. Clay and Calhoun somehow got the curious idea that Van Buren was even more than a Gray Eminence, that he was the real brains of the Jackson administration. They reasoned that if they could hit Van Buren they would paralyze Jackson. So they hit him.

Congress had adjourned before Van Buren was made minister to England under what is called a recess appointment. He went to London, took up his post, and had been there for months before the Senate came back to Washington. But when it did, Clay and Calhoun persuaded their followers to refuse to confirm the nomination on the ground that Van Buren was a notoriously unfit person.

This action left him in a terribly embarrassing position in London, and he was furious. But on his way home he thought the matter over and changed his tactics. When he landed in New York the newspaper men found him smiling, cheerful, and apparently not at all upset. He pointed out what everybody suspected: that the Senators were not gunning for him, but for the President. If by taking this blow he could prevent Jackson from being hurt, it was right and proper that he should do so.

Most of the country, including Andrew Jackson, said, "Why, the fellow's a good sport!" and he became so popular that he was easily elected Vice-President in 1832 and President in 1836. Van Buren took over the Jackson Cabinet, except that he made Joel Poinsett Secretary of War, but he asked and expected nothing new of it.

Then in 1837 Van Buren's luck ran out. A money panic struck the country, largely on account of Jackson's failure to find a substitute for the Bank of the United States, and the Democrats were beaten in 1840.

What with the panic of 1837 and various minor mistakes, the Democratic party was in real trouble, and it seemed that any Whig candidate was bound to win. Now was the time for Clay but his arro-

gance backfired. Thurlow Weed was a New York
politician twice as slick as Van Buren had ever
been. In fact, he took control of New York away
from Van Buren and elected a Whig governor. But
Henry Clay brushed Weed aside, as he had
brushed aside too many other Whigs, so Weed
organized these disgruntled politicians. Together
they nominated William Henry Harrison, an old,
retired general of the War of 1812, honest enough,
but without a political idea in his head.

That strategy stopped Clay, but Weed wasn't
sure he could elect Harrison without some Democratic votes, so he looked about for a Democrat
who hated Jackson to run as the Vice-Presidential
candidate. There were plenty of such Democrats,
and he decided on a Virginian named John Tyler,
who had supported Clay. Clay swallowed his dis-
appointment and worked for the ticket. It won
easily.

Harrison offered to make Clay Secretary of
State, but he preferred to remain in the Senate.
Without a doubt he believed that as leader of the
Senate he could manage the old general and make
Thurlow Weed sick of his own scheme. Harrison
then made Daniel Webster Secretary of State, no
doubt with Clay's approval, because that left Clay

master of the Whig party in the Senate. The rest of
the Cabinet was filled with strong Clay men, and
at least two of them, John Bell, Secretary of War,
and John J. Crittenden, Attorney General were
better-than-average officials.

But the maneuvering was all to no purpose. In
the bitter weather of his Inauguration Day the new
President caught cold and couldn't throw it off.
Eventually it developed into pneumonia, and he
died on April 4, 1841, having been President exactly one month.

Never before had a President died in office, and
immediately the question arose, what did John
Tyler become? The Constitution didn't say. It
provided that in case of the death of a President his
duties should "devolve upon" the Vice-President.
That wording certainly made him Acting President, but what more and for how long? For the
rest of the term? Until a special election could be
called? Or what? Everybody had an opinion, but
there was no general agreement.

One man, however, was certain, and that man
was Tyler. The first official document that came
for his signature after Harrison's death he signed,
"John Tyler, President of the United States." And
that was that. Argument raged for years, but no-

body knew what to do about it, and nothing was done. From that time on, whenever a President has died, the Vice-President has become President for the remainder of the term.

Two things about this event are worth noting. In the first place, Tyler established a precedent that in a crisis when plainly something has to be done, the President takes the power and does it, whether anyone is sure that he rightfully has the power or not. If he is mistaken, and neither Congress nor the Supreme Court can correct the mistake, the people can do it by amending the Constitution. But it has been proved again and again that if the President acts promptly, and what he does is sensible, even if not ideal, the people will back him. This fact worries those who believe that everything must be done strictly according to rules made long ago, but the American system works in this way, and nobody has been able to change it.

In the second place, Tyler's prompt decision to be President, not Acting President, should have warned Clay, but it didn't. He thought it meant nothing much, because he had made up his mind that Tyler was nothing much. "I'll drive him before me," he said. He did not realize that something had been added to the former Senator from Virginia. That something was the Presidency. John Tyler as a Senator may have been nothing much, but the same man as President of the United States was a great deal.

Clay, therefore, without consulting Tyler, set about undoing much of what Jackson had done. In particular he proposed to set up the Bank of the United States again, exactly as it was before. Tyler, as a matter of fact, rather favored a bank, but not one just like the old one; he insisted on more government control. Clay paid no attention. He rammed through Congress a bill written according to his own ideas, and Tyler instantly vetoed it. Clay came back with another, modified slightly, but not enough. Tyler vetoed that one, too.

Tyler had taken over Harrison's Cabinet as it stood. After the second veto of the Bank bill, Clay ordered all members to resign, thinking that a mass resignation would ruin Tyler.

But he was doing more than that. He was asserting that the Cabinet must take orders from Congress rather than from the President. This principle would have altered our whole system of government, for it would have established the rule that the legislative can control the executive, and our system is that each branch must be independent of the other two. Congress, for the third time, was attempting to alter this balance.

Nevertheless, all the Cabinet members resigned except the Secretary of State. Daniel Webster had no great liking for Tyler, but he liked still less being ordered around by Henry Clay. Besides, he was busy with an important treaty with England, fixing the northern boundary of the State of Maine. It was a tricky business at best, and to walk out in the middle of the argument would have ruined everything. So he informed Clay that when he had finished his treaty he would get out, but not before. He stayed until 1843 when the Webster-Ashburton treaty was concluded.

Tyler managed to fill the Cabinet, although with not very distinguished men. The best of the lot was probably Abel P. Upshur, whom at first he made Secretary of the Navy, then, when Webster resigned, Secretary of State. But in 1844 Upshur was killed by the explosion of a big naval gun, which he was watching being tested on a warship. Then Tyler gave the Department of State to John C. Calhoun, Clay's chief enemy.

Calhoun, a Southerner and a strong proslavery man, took one very important step while Secretary

of State. With the aid of President Tyler he drove through Congress a joint resolution admitting Texas to the Union on the last day of February, 1845. Up to that time nothing had been done about its application, because acceptance meant trouble with Mexico and also the acquisition of more slave territory. On March 4 Tyler's term ended, and James K. Polk became the ninth President of the United States.

Polk is sometimes described as the most successful of all Presidents. The excuse for this statement is that before taking office he announced that he proposed to do five things, and he did all five. No one can beat a batting average of one thousand.

His five proposals were: first, to acquire California; second, to secure full control of Oregon, including what is now the State of Washington, then held jointly with the British; third, to lower the tariff; fourth, to set up a subtreasury system as a substitute for the Bank of the United States; and, fifth, to retire at the end of his first term.

What he did not expect to do was to fight a war with Mexico, but he was quite prepared to do so if Mexico made any attempt to regain Texas. Mexico did, and the war followed in 1846. Mexico was battered into agreeing to sell California, for which Polk paid her as much as Jefferson had paid for the whole Louisiana territory. The fighting mood of the United States may have helped persuade Great Britain to settle the Oregon boundary, and so Polk also disposed of this matter in 1846.

One result of the Mexican War was to make the War Department more military and less political. Up to this time the country had depended on soldiers who were more or less amateurs, and we had developed a notion that there really wasn't much to the art of war, that any prominent citizen could command an army. Washington, who won the Revolution, Jackson, who won the battle of New Orleans, Harrison, who won the battles of Tippecanoe and the Thames, had all been part-time soldiers. So when the Mexican War broke out many prominent politicians—Senator Thomas Hart Benton, of Missouri, for one example—expected to command armies.

But General Winfield Scott, the chief of staff, was a professional soldier, and he said no. He said that it took a man trained to the art to hold a high command. He and Secretary of War, William L. Marcy, quarreled constantly, and Scott could have been dismissed for some of the things he said.

However, Zachary Taylor, who was a professional even if he did ride around the battlefield in a straw hat and a checked gingham shirt, soon defeated the Mexican army of northern Mexico; and Scott, taking the chief field command himself, fought his way from Veracruz all the way up to Mexico City in a campaign without a serious military mistake anywhere.

Scott's success almost settled the question, and the Civil War, fifteen years later, did settle it. Since then the Secretary of War has been strictly a behind-the-lines official. He is the final authority in that he can say who shall command, but he no longer tries to say how he shall command. That decision is left to the professional.

Zachary Taylor came home a national hero, although Scott really won the war. But the better soldier is not always the more popular man. The difference in their popularity was shown by their nicknames. Taylor, in his straw hat, was called Old Rough-and-Ready. Scott, in his correct military uniform, was called Old Fuss-and-Feathers. In 1848 Scott was left to command the Army, but Taylor was elected President.

He lived long enough to establish a new department, that of the Interior, but he died in 1850, after being President only sixteen months, and his Vice-President, Millard Fillmore, became President without serious opposition.

Franklin Pierce, the fourteenth and often called the most obscure of all Presidents, gained that low reputation because his administration faced no great problems and therefore solved none. During these years, from 1852 to 1856, the Whig party went to pieces. It had become too much a one-man affair, and the one man, Henry Clay, was now dead. So were Webster and Calhoun, and the great statesmen who were to follow them had not yet appeared.

So the country droned on through Pierce's administration, and that of his successor, James Buchanan, with no marked change. It was not that there were no problems. The greatest and most terrible of all was looming up, but Pierce, and especially Buchanan, refused to face it. This problem concerned Negro slavery, and it came nearer than any other to destroying the country.

Since the Democratic party would not face the issue, and the Whig party had collapsed, a new party that would take a straight look at slavery was formed and opposed Buchanan in 1856. It was defeated, but four years later came back with another candidate, who won because the Democratic party split three ways. This man was to prove himself one of the greatest—some say flatly the greatest—of all Presidents. He was Abraham Lincoln, who, among his other achievements, gave the Cabinet a completely new look.

TEAM OF WILD ANIMALS

Lincoln is such a great name today that we are likely to think that it was always so. But in 1860 it meant very little. At that time most people believed that the biggest man in the new Republican party was William H. Seward, a Senator from New York, and nobody was more certain of his importance than Senator Seward. However, a certain number of people said no, the really big Republican was Salmon P. Chase, governor of Ohio, and Governor Chase agreed heartily.

At the beginning of 1860 very few paid much attention to Abraham Lincoln. He was admitted to be a pretty good speaker in a plain fashion, but not in the rolling thunder style of Daniel Webster. In 1858 the nation had been startled by this country

lawyer's campaign against the biggest man in the
Democratic party, Stephen A. Douglas, for the
Senatorship from Illinois. Lincoln lost, as was expected; as was *not* expected, his campaign argument drove Douglas into a corner, and to get out
he had to make statements that enraged Democrats, mostly Southern, who favored slavery. Two
years later these statements were used to split
the Democratic party. The Northern Democrats
named Douglas, but the Southerners nominated a
Kentuckian named Breckinridge, while a splinter
group named Bell, from Tennessee. Together these
three got 944,109 more popular votes than Lincoln,
but they won only 123 electoral votes, while he
had 180 and needed only 152 to win.

Lincoln's party, though, was not a real party. It
was a bundle of groups bound together by one
string—the fact that they all believed in the Union.
There were the old-line Whigs, who called Seward
their chief, now that Clay was dead. There were
the new Abolitionists, who followed Chase. There
were various splinters—Know-Nothings, Free Soil-
ers, Anti-Masons, and others—that had been combined by a shrewd and tricky politician in Pennsylvania, Simon Cameron. Finally, in the border
states, there were many Democrats, such as Ed-

ward Bates, of Missouri, who opposed slavery, but disliked Douglas. All these types voted for Lincoln, but for different reasons.

When the national convention met in Chicago most people assumed that Seward would be nominated, although Chase, Cameron, Bates, and Lincoln all had delegates. But Seward had made many enemies in the past, and the feeling grew that if he were nominated the Democrats would forget their quarrels and combine to beat him. The same thing was true of Chase. Then on the second ballot Cameron suddenly threw the Pennsylvania delegation to Lincoln, and on the third ballot there was a stampede to him, and he was nominated.

When the election had been won and Lincoln announced his Cabinet, he included the four men who had run against him in the convention—Seward as Secretary of State, Chase as Secretary of the Treasury, Cameron as Secretary of War, and Bates as Attorney General.

To many people Lincoln seemed to have done a crazy thing. What? Fill up the Cabinet with men each of whom thought he, and not Lincoln, ought to be President? If that were not enough, each of the four had reasons for hating the others as well as Lincoln. Everyone knew that Seward thought

that Cameron had cheated him out of the nomination. Everyone knew that Chase was equally certain that Seward and Cameron had ganged up to
cheat *him* out of the nomination. Bates wasn't even
a Republican, and more than once he had said
publicly that he had little respect for Seward,
Chase, and Cameron.

Many shrewd observers believed that no man
on earth could make that gang work together, certainly not this rail-splitter from Illinois. Lincoln
seemed to be asking for trouble, and it occurred to
few that the four, held together under Lincoln's
eye, would be less dangerous than they would be
working against him out of sight.

The other three places in the Cabinet also
seemed to be oddly distributed. The Postmaster
General was Montgomery Blair, not well known
nationally but strong in Missouri. His father, Fran-
cis P. Blair, was even stronger in Maryland. Both
states were critical in the struggle that was taking
shape. The Secretary of the Navy was another ex-
Democrat, Gideon Welles, of Connecticut. He was
hated by Seward, Chase, and Cameron, and he
hated them just as heartily. The Secretary of the
Interior was Caleb B. Smith, of Indiana, of whom

most people knew nothing, because as a matter of fact there was nothing much to know.

With this outfit Lincoln faced the almost certain threat of civil war. It is not surprising that all kinds of men expected the government to fly to pieces in less than six months.

However, these gloomy prophets did not consider carefully enough that Lincoln's first job was to make a party out of a bundle of splinters; therefore, each splinter had to have at least one representative in the Cabinet. They also overlooked that five of these men, vain and cantankerous as they all were, each had one thing that he could do supremely well. A sixth man, Cameron, was at least a master schemer.

Most importantly, Abraham Lincoln knew that he had not only the title of President, but the ability to be President. He alone had no doubt that, given the authority to do so, he could boss any seven men in the country, even if they included such men as Seward, Chase, Bates, Welles, and Blair. Two years later, when someone came to Lincoln and told him flatly that Seward was trying to take the government away from him, Lincoln answered quietly, "Seward knows I am his master." At that time, perhaps, Seward didn't, but Lincoln did, and eventually Seward found out.

When he first entered the Cabinet and before he had learned what a man Lincoln really was, Seward had a notion that he was to be the real power. The first jolt came when he found that he would not be allowed to name the other members of the Cabinet, and the second when he found that he could not dictate the policies of the administration.

The curious thing is that when he did discover that Lincoln was the master, this haughty and tricky man took it very well.

For one thing he had a sense of humor. He could see the point of Lincoln's jokes, as such solemn fellows as Chase and Bates and Welles never could. In the second place, before the end of the first term Seward realized that the Republican party would have to renominate Lincoln or give away the election, so he had no part in the scheme to defeat Lincoln in the convention. The outcome was that as time passed Lincoln and Seward began to enjoy each other's company and became real friends.

Two men, Cameron and Smith, had been forced on Lincoln by foolish deals that his friends, contrary to his instructions, had made to secure votes in the nominating convention. Cameron had a bad reputation before he entered the Cabinet, and the first year of the war made it worse. Scandal after scandal in connection with the purchase of supplies for the Army made it appear that Cameron was using his position to make his friends rich at the expense of the country. Yet to fire Cameron outright would have enraged Pennsylvania, so Lincoln got rid of him by making him minister to Russia.

Cameron was replaced with the queerest character in Lincoln's collection of oddities. He was Edwin M. Stanton, generally regarded as the finest trial lawyer in the country, but given at times to such strange behavior that there were serious doubts of his sanity. In time of trouble he was given to hysterics. When his first child, a baby girl, died, Stanton had the body placed in a metal casket and kept it on the mantelpiece in his bedroom for several years. After his first wife died, he placed her nightcap and gown on the bed every night and sat there for hours, weeping. By a dozen other freakish acts he made men wonder if he had kept all his wits. He was a tremendous hater, but he was also a tremendous worker. He knew how to drive the men under him, and he would not steal.

Despite these facts, Lincoln's Cabinet was a very fine one. Seward was vain, shifty, and sometimes downright insolent to his chief; but he was a great Secretary of State. Chase was vainer, shiftier, and more insolent than Seward, but he managed the Treasury splendidly. Bates looked on the others with contempt, but he was a first-rate Attorney General. Welles hated everybody except Lincoln, but he was honest, loyal, and ran the Navy department efficiently. Stanton despised Lincoln and did all he could to block his renomination; but he swept the crooks out of the War Department and kept the staff on their toes. Blair's explosions of temper—and even more those of the old politician his father and of his brother, Frank, a general in the Union Army—were always giving trouble, but he was a steadfast friend of Lincoln and handled the post office well.

This Cabinet was the first one to begin to understand the actual status of the United States Constitution. Driven by necessity, it abandoned the idea that the Constitution was a kind of steel framework within which the government must be kept confined. Lincoln's Cabinet saw "the supreme law of the land" as a blueprint, showing lines along which the government might be expanded and extended as the country grew and changed. These years, therefore, were the ones that made the Cabinet what it is today. The change was bound to come, because the country was changing, but it was speeded up by the influence of a great President.

Looking back, we can see that the one great fault of the Lincoln Cabinet was that it did not understand the real greatness of Abraham Lincoln until he was dead.

The politicians in Congress did not understand Lincoln's greatness either. They had set up a Committee on the Conduct of the War—Cameron's scandals had much to do with that—which, by its constant meddling with military affairs, came close to losing the war. But the members didn't realize that. They patted themselves on the back for having saved the country from the blunders of that foolish man, Lincoln, and they were still strutting when, right after the final victory, Lincoln was murdered.

Andrew Johnson, the Vice-President, assumed the title of President in 1865 without any argument. However, although Congress, openly abetted by certain members of the Cabinet, allowed him to have the title they had no idea of allowing him to be President in fact.

Before his death Lincoln had outlined a plan for

clearing away the wreckage left by the war, and Johnson undertook to put that plan into effect. But the extremists in Congress considered the program too easy on the South, so they determined to set it aside and substitute one of their own.

This effort of the legislative to take over the executive branch of the government was the fourth, the greatest, and the most nearly successful. It was led by Thaddeus Stevens, of Pennsylvania, in the House, and by Charles Sumner, of Massachusetts, in the Senate. The line that they followed was the same that Clay had followed. It was to make the Cabinet responsible to Congress instead of the President.

Stevens and Sumner expected little trouble, for nobody regarded Johnson as half the man that Lincoln had been. However, he proved to be a stubborn and a bold, if not very skillful, fighter. He had no intention of giving up his authority to Congress, and when Stanton, having become an ally of Stevens and Sumner, flatly refused to obey an order of the President, Johnson fired him and appointed General Grant Secretary of War. Congress responded in 1868 by impeaching the President and attempting to remove him, an effort that failed by just one vote in the Senate.

This row took up the rest of Johnson's term. The legislative was defeated when impeachment failed, but Congress vented its spite by passing what is known as the Tenure of Office Act, making it unlawful for the President to dismiss a member of the Cabinet without the consent of the Senate. Many lawyers think that this act was unconstitutional, but it was repealed some twenty years later without ever having been tested in the Supreme Court.

Seward and Welles, survivors of the Lincoln Cabinet, stayed with Johnson to the end, and during this period Seward made his finest stroke of diplomacy by buying Alaska from the Russians. He got small credit at the time. His critics were scornful of what they called Seward's folly, for few had any idea of how valuable Alaska was to be, or that its purchase would be remembered as the wisest act of that Secretary of State.

THE CABINET GROWS

Ulysses S. Grant was elected President in 1868. He had been a fine soldier, but that didn't make him a fine President. Apparently he regarded the office as a reward for his wartime services rather than as a job far more laborious and complicated than that of commanding an army.

Grant sought to enjoy the office, and so he did not run it. Knowing nothing about politics, he allowed a collection of scamps to slip into high offices and had to fire one after another, with great embarrassment. He had a total of twenty-five men to fill seven offices in the Cabinet, and it sank to what is probably the lowest level it ever reached in public respect.

There was one important change under Grant.

In 1870 the Department of Justice was established, and the Attorney General, who at first was merely the President's legal adviser, became the chief law officer of the government and the head of an executive department.

The Grant administration exposed the great weakness of a system in which Congress controlled the Cabinet. After what happened to Andrew Johnson, Grant had little wish to do battle with Congress, not even to remain master in his own house. But the result was not what Congressmen expected. When the President gave up effective control, it did not go to Congress; instead, it slipped into the hands of various outsiders whom Grant happened to like. Some of these men were far from honest, and the advice they gave the President was bad. The outcome was almost, perhaps quite, the worst administration in American history.

The explanation is easy. In the actual operation of the government, that is, the jobs that have to be done every day in order to keep things moving, it is necessary for somebody to tell the workers what to do and when to do it. As the government grows bigger and the number of workers increases, more and more sub bosses are required, and the man at the top knows less and less about what the men at

the bottom are doing. Therefore, it is essential for him to hold the sub bosses to strict account. If the President tries to share this authority with Congress, it will simply slip away altogether and nobody will be in control.

Terrible proof of this eventuality was furnished by what happened from 1868 to 1876. When Lincoln's plan for restoring the Union was scrapped, nothing took its place. It was not that there was no other plan. There were too many. Everybody had his own, and each planner insisted that his was the only one that could work. They ranged from the extreme radicals' idea that the Civil War had detroyed the Union by wiping out the Southern states, to the extreme conservatives' idea that the thing to do was to pretend that there never had been a war and go back to 1860.

Today most historians agree that none of these plans was as sound as Lincoln's original program although any one of them—except the hopeless ideas of the extremists on both ends—might have worked after a fashion. But none could be applied, because Congress could not settle on what it wanted. So things drifted from bad to worse until by 1876 conditions in the Southern states were dreadful.

Then the voters revolted and, in the election of 1876, gave Tilden, the Democratic candidate, 250,-000 more votes than they gave Hayes, the Republican. If the electoral votes of three Southern states were thrown out, however, Hayes would have a majority of one in the electoral college. By a scheme of doubtful legality they were thrown out, and Hayes became President. Of course, he was charged with having made a corrupt deal, but the charges have never been proved. He did, however, abandon all further efforts at what was called Reconstruction—ironically, for nothing had really been reconstructed—in the South.

After that time there was no strong, determined effort by the legislative to take over the executive. Congress forever quarreled with the President, and often blocked what he wanted to do, but it did not try seriously to take over his job.

The Cabinet came to be recognized as a group of men to whom the President delegated as much of his authority as each needed in order to run his department. In other words, they were the President's agents. Some Cabinet members were great men, but they were the President's men as long as they stayed in the Cabinet. When they became anything else, they either got out or were thrown out.

In 1886 Grover Cleveland, who was then the President, informed Congress that he regarded the Tenure of Office Act as unconstitutional, therefore no law, and he would pay no attention to it. He urged Congress to repeal it.

Congress did so, in 1887, for when members considered the matter calmly there was nothing else to do. Congress cannot give orders to the President about what he is to do within his own branch of the government. It can only impeach and remove him, and to do that it must prove that he is guilty of "treason, bribery, or other high crimes and misdemeanors." A high crime or misdemeanor is one that is very serious; merely disagreeing with Congress on a point of law could not possibly be considered a high crime.

So the legislative branch yielded, and the Tenure of Office Act was repealed. But the repeal really didn't make much difference because a strong President will rule his Cabinet anyhow, and a weak one is more likely to lose control to some political boss than to Congress.

Grover Cleveland also expanded the Cabinet during his administration. By this time the work of providing food for all the people had become so important that the government had hired many experts to do nothing but study how to grow the crops best suited to each section of the country. President Cleveland put these men into a Department of Agriculture and added a Secretary of Agriculture to his Cabinet.

In 1894 Richard Olney, Cleveland's Attorney General, played a part in determining an important government policy. Undoubtedly he persuaded the President to send Federal troops into Chicago over the protest of the governor of Illinois, to break a strike against the Pullman Company. This decision was perhaps the worst mistake of Cleveland's career.

Still another memorable act of the Cleveland administration was the establishment of the Interstate Commerce Commission. The law was enacted under Article I, section 8, paragraph 3 of the Constitution, giving Congress power "to regulate commerce with foreign nations and among the several states." However, to regulate is not exactly a legislative, an executive, or a judicial function. It is all three. A regulator makes rules (legislative), enforces them (executive), and decides how they shall apply in a given case (judicial).

The need for regulation means that the doctrine of separation of powers holds good up to a certain point, but beyond that point the powers simply can't be separated and no doctrine or theory can do it. That point is where one finishes laying down rules and begins regulating conduct. The United States reached it when the Interstate Commerce Commission was established in 1887. Its chief business was to see that the railroads treated everybody fairly, in which it was quite successful, and it was the first of what are called the independent agencies that have multiplied until today they have taken a large part of the government's business out of the hands of the President's Cabinet.

Nevertheless, the number of posts in the Cabinet continued to increase, because the number of things the American government had to look after also increased. Under Theodore Roosevelt a Department of Commerce and Labor was created, and the secretary joined the Cabinet. Under Woodrow Wilson the department was split into two, and so there were a Secretary of Commerce and a Secretary of Labor.

Politics played an important part in Wilson's choice of Cabinet members. He had little sympathy with most of William J. Bryan's political views, but Bryan had millions of devoted followers whose support Wilson had to have. So he made Bryan Secretary of State, perhaps on the ground that Bryan's views on domestic affairs could not affect foreign policy. But when war broke out in 1914, Bryan turned into such an intense pacifist that he and Wilson could not get along; so the Secretary resigned. This break, though, was a matter of principle, not a personal quarrel, and on domestic issues Bryan continued to give Wilson all the help he could.

Harding's Cabinet was the most extraordinary of recent years. It included Charles E. Hughes, Secretary of State, and Herbert Hoover, Secretary of Commerce, both men of great ability and high character. It also included Albert B. Fall, Secretary of the Interior, and Harry M. Daugherty, Attorney General. Later Fall went to jail and Daugherty might have gone had not someone burned the records on which the government expected to convict him. Nobody thinks that Harding took part in the crooked work, and the usual explanation is that he was betrayed by his friends, but he was really betrayed by his own unfitness for the job.

Franklin D. Roosevelt, the only man four times elected to the Presidency, recruited a Kitchen Cabinet under the name of the Brains Trust before he ever reached the White House. It was a group of specialists in various subjects, most of them drawn from universities. As university professors were supposed to be brainy, newspaper reporters said Roosevelt was trying to monopolize all the brains in the country—hence, the Brains Trust.

Roosevelt also set precedent by naming as Secretary of Labor Frances Perkins, the first woman ever to sit in the Cabinet. Later, when war seemed to be inevitable, he named a Republican, Henry L. Stimson, Secretary of War, and another, Frank Knox, Secretary of the Navy. Both, incidentally, served him loyally.

But Roosevelt was an exception to all rules. He had flaming rows with members both of the regular Cabinet and the Brains Trust. Several quit and thereafter fought him, openly and furiously, and they fought among themselves through all the twelve years of his Presidency. But if any ever plotted against him secretly and tried to stab him in the back, as they stabbed John Adams, the fact has never been discovered.

During Harry Truman's administration, the War Department and the Navy Department, were combined, with the Air Force, into one Department of Defense. Under Dwight Eisenhower, a Department of Health, Education, and Welfare was created, and its secretary was added to the Cabinet.

Eisenhower followed Roosevelt's example by appointing one Democrat, Martin P. Durkin, as Secretary of Labor in his original Cabinet. But it didn't work; Durkin soon resigned. President John F. Kennedy also named two Republicans, Robert S. McNamara to Defense, and C. Douglas Dillon to the Treasury, and these appointments *did* work. President Lyndon B. Johnson kept both until Dillon resigned for nonpolitical reasons. Perhaps finance and military affairs will be regarded henceforth as nonpartisan departments. President Johnson also expanded the Cabinet by creating a Department of Housing and Urban Development in 1965.

The Cabinet as it stands is clearly in process of change, and it will change not in accordance with anyone's plans or wishes, but as events compel it to. Therefore, to predict exactly what it is going to be is risky, but a few new developments are beginning to make themselves clear.

THE CABINET IN THE FUTURE

The expansion of the Cabinet means that the President has to consult with more advisers all the time. Some years back President Truman appointed ex-President Hoover head of a commission to find out what could be done to organize the executive branch efficiently. The Hoover Commission made recommendations, a few of which have been put into effect. However, there is no solution to the chief difficulty, which is that the ordinary business of government is now so gigantic that a large number of very able men are required to keep it moving at all.

There is another objection to simplifying the government that politicians do not like to talk about, but it is important. It is that where confusion exists smart fellows can put over more easily schemes of their own that give them more power and profit than they are entitled to, so they like confusion and oppose reform.

At best, the heads of departments and independent agencies, which is to say, the great officers of state, are already too many to form an intimate group of advisers, and they are certain to increase in number. Already the Cabinet, to a large extent, is reduced to a directorate that meets with the President mainly to report on the routine conduct of affairs. It could not be otherwise. The Secretary of the Interior, for example, has a tremendous job in his own department. How can he advise on whether or not an expeditionary force should be sent to some remote corner of the world where fighting has broken out and American interests and lives are in danger? Or how can the Secretary of Health, Education, and Welfare be expected to know the political effect on India of the Treasury Department's silver-purchasing policy? If each member handles his own department efficiently, he is doing all that may reasonably be required of him.

Yet no really big problem affects only one department, and the enormous ones—the issue of war or peace, for example—affect them all. In such cases the advice of the various secretaries, each thinking of his own department, is almost sure to be contradictory, and the President must make the final decision. But he is foolish if he does not seek the best counsel available, and whether the man who gives it holds a great office, a small one, or none at all doesn't matter.

Therefore, something like Jackson's much-derided Kitchen Cabinet exists and has existed for many years, especially when the President is a strong man full of original ideas. Also the shadowy figure of the Gray Eminence has become more familiar to Americans. Again and again some man has been picked by Washington's gossips as such an adviser. He never holds any important office, sometimes none at all. But if the President trusts him and values his judgment he may count for more than the Secretary of State. He is most likely to appear when politics forces the President to appoint to the Cabinet men who are lukewarm toward some of his pet projects. Mark Hanna was regarded as the Gray Eminence to William McKinley, Colonel House to Woodrow Wilson, Harry Hopkins to Franklin D. Roosevelt.

There are serious objections to such men holding great power. After all, ours is supposed to be

the people's government, and the people have a
right to know who is running it in their name. Yet
the President must not be denied full opportunity
to consult any man on anything, if he has reason
to believe that the man is wise and especially well-
informed. We never think of objecting to such con-
sultation on relatively small matters. When a man
who has made an important discovery, or read
some ancient language never before translated, or
performed an extraordinary feat, is invited to the
White House to tell what he knows, everybody ap-
proves. Surely, we should approve even more
heartily when the President calls in wise men to
advise him on supremely important matters of national policy. Frequently it is also necessary for the
President to seek the advice of men who have time
to examine the whole picture, not one small frag-
ment of it, and men who are already responsible
for managing a vast department have not time
enough to consider the overall situation. For these
reasons every President has some unofficial advisers.

Since the President is going to get unofficial advice anyhow, it might be wise to arrange to have
him do so under fixed rules known to everyone.
Perhaps the Kitchen Cabinet should be supplanted

with a genuine council of state. The people cannot rule themselves successfully unless they know exactly what they are doing or, rather, what is being done in their name. In any government, if the real power is hidden, so that nobody knows exactly who has done what, democracy is impossible.

There are few things that a government really needs to do secretly. It cannot tell the world its military plans, and its diplomats sometimes learn facts that, if published, would do harm to some friendly nation. In these cases secrecy is right and proper. But military affairs and diplomatic plots are a small part of all government operations; the routine business is vastly greater, and it is the routine business that directly affects the people. The taxes that are levied, the laws that are passed, the money that is spent on nonmilitary activities are the people's business and the people are entitled to know all about them.

Consider, for example, a new law that either enlarges or restricts the citizen's rights. If the people are to judge it correctly, one of the first things they need to know is, whose idea was it?

There are arguments both for and against making a President's advisers official. If they are not responsible for a department, they still should be responsible for the advice they give the President. In some countries—Great Britain, for example— this question has been answered by appointment of what are known as "ministers without portfolio." Their sole duty is to advise the prime minister, but they have the rank and draw the salaries of other ministers and, which is the really important thing, they are known to everybody.

Every President needs an expert to advise him on party politics. For years the custom was to make him the Postmaster General, or occasionally the Attorney General. But both of these Cabinet officers have big departments to run. Why should not the politician-in-chief be recognized for what he is, rather than be called the head of a department that other people must run while he studies politics?

In recent years it has been said of every strong President that he was his own Secretary of State. That judgment is not proof that the secretaries have been incompetent. All it means is that when the President is trying to figure how to deal with the Russians he cannot always expect sound advice from a man who spends much of his time worrying over who shall be ambassador to Guatemala or Siam. We have tried to remedy this situation by making the undersecretary the real head of the department, but that solution has not worked any too well. It is a way of dodging around the question instead of answering it.

The objection to recognizing the Kitchen Cabinet as a real council of state is that an official cannot be fired without creating a great uproar in Congress and the country. Not all men are equally good advisers in all circumstances, so the Kitchen Cabinet has always been subject to rapid changes that, as long as the group is unofficial, pass without much notice.

Be that as it may, plainly the Cabinet is in a process of change, and what it is to become is anybody's guess. Because the Constitution never said what it should be, it can be anything that seems necessary. Washington made it a council of state. Jackson made it a false front behind which the real work was done. Lincoln made it a team of wild animals harnessed and driven by one tremendously strong man. Most modern Presidents have made it a bunch of superintendents—the statelier term is "primarily an administrative organization."

But what the next President, or the next half-dozen Presidents, will make it, nobody knows. All depends on the strength and wisdom of the man in control, and his ability depends on the good sense that the people show in choosing a President. If they elect a man who is strong and wise, the Cabinet will be a fine instrument of government; if he is foolish and weak, the Cabinet will explode as it did under Andrew Johnson.

The final responsibility rests with us, which is exactly what the men who founded the government intended.

Members of the Cabinet of President Dwight D. Eisenhower

Secretary of State
John Foster Dulles
Christian A. Herter

Secretary of the Treasury
George M. Humphrey
Robert B. Anderson

Secretary of Defense
Charles E. Wilson
Neil H. McElroy
Thomas S. Gates

Attorney General
H. Brownell, Jr.
William P. Rogers

Postmaster General
A. E. Summerfield

Secretary of the Interior
Douglas McKay
Fred A. Seaton

Secretary of Agriculture
Ezra Taft Benson

Secretary of Labor
Martin P. Durkin
James P. Mitchell

Secretary of Commerce
Sinclair Weeks
Lewis L. Strauss
Frederick H. Mueller

Secretary of Health, Education, and Welfare
Oveta Culp Hobby
Marion B. Folsom
Arthur S. Flemming

Members of the Cabinet of
President John F. Kennedy

Secretary of State
Dean Rusk

Secretary of the Treasury
C. Douglas Dillon

Secretary of Defense
Robert S. McNamara

Attorney General
Robert F. Kennedy

Postmaster General
J. Edward Day
John A. Gronouski

Secretary of the Interior
Stewart L. Udall

Secretary of Agriculture
Orville L. Freeman

Secretary of Labor
Arthur J. Goldberg
William Willard Wirtz

Secretary of Commerce
Luther H. Hodges

Secretary of Health, Education, and Welfare
Abraham A. Ribicoff
Anthony J. Celebrezze

Members of the Cabinet of President Lyndon B. Johnson

Secretary of State
Dean Rusk

Secretary of the Treasury
C. Douglas Dillon
Henry H. Fowler

Secretary of Defense
Robert S. McNamara

Attorney General
Robert F. Kennedy
Nicholas de B. Katzenbach

Postmaster General
John A. Gronouski
Lawrence F. O'Brien

Secretary of the Interior
Stewart L. Udall

Secretary of Agriculture
Orville L. Freeman

Secretary of Labor
William Willard Wirtz

Secretary of Commerce
John T. Connor

Secretary of Health, Education, and Welfare
Anthony J. Celebrezze

Secretary of the Air Force
Eugene M. Zuckert

Secretary of the Army
Stephen Ailes

Secretary of the Navy
Paul H. Nitze

Secretary of Housing and Urban Development

INDEX

Indicates illustrations